W9-AHJ-225

*The Secret Life of*
# JOHN PAUL II

# *The Secret Life of* JOHN PAUL II

Lino Zani

*With*

Marilù Simoneschi

*Translated by*

Matthew Sherry

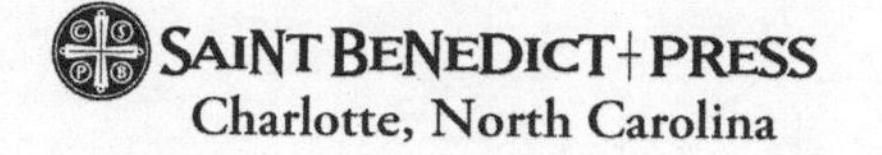

English Translation by Matthew Sherry.



Cover design by Chris Pelicano.

Cover photos used with permission. Courtesy of L'Osservatore Romano (PhotoVat.com).

Cataloging-in-Publication data on file with the Library of Congress.

ISBN: 978-1-61890-404-1

Published in the United States by
Saint Benedict Press, LLC
P.O. Box 410487
Charlotte, NC 28241
www.saintbenedictpress.com

Printed and bound in the United States of America.

# TABLE OF CONTENTS


Prologue . . . . . . . . . . . . . . . . . . . . vii

I On the Trail of a Secret . . . . . . . . . . . . . . 1

II A Good "Refuge" for the Pope . . . . . . . . . 21

III Two Friends on the Snow: The Pope and Pertini . . . . . . . . . . . . . 37

IV The Silence of Prayer . . . . . . . . . . . . . . 51

V Signs of Holiness . . . . . . . . . . . . . . . . 89

VI A Cross of Granite That Touches the Sky . 139

VII Praying at the North Pole . . . . . . . . . . 163

Chronology of Events . . . . . . . . . . . . 185

# PROLOGUE

THAT Pope John Paul II loved the mountains and fully identified with the peace of that world is well known. What is not so well known is that there is an eyewitness to his exceptional relationship with that part of creation. His name is Lino Zani, at first the pontiff's skiing instructor and alpine guide, and then, little by little over the years, a friend whom John Paul spiritually accompanied on attempts at the summits.

The pope's love of the mountains was present throughout his life, in its active and contemplative phases. It was a solitary love, an intense love—but one always imbued with all the personality and holiness of the man who, with his witness of faith, shook the conscience of the world.

Here Zani shares with us never before published stories of John Paul II: Stories of days and nights, of human emotions and exchanges, on which Zani observed silence for years, but that now, on the verge of the imminent beatification of John Paul II, he intends to unravel. Here he beautifully shares with the whole world the privilege of his friendship with a pope who was acclaimed, from the very day of his death, to be *Santo Subito!* (one who should be canonized immediately).

And then there is a "secret" of the pope. Something that no one has ever unveiled. The story that you are about to read recounts the mystical experiences through which John Paul developed —in a complete and clear manner—the awareness of finding himself at the center of a "prodigious" event. *Him*, in a vision presented by the Virgin to the shepherds of Fatima, *him* in the midst of the unfolding of events that would play out over an entire century.

Finally, there is the dramatic impact of certain events and the apparent "coincidence" that would take him to the snowy slopes of Mount Adamello. Before him, a "little paradise" overlapped with—and in sharp contrast to—the images of an "infernal" tableau: That of the First World War, a past of death and hatred, a hatred that would return many years later to make an attempt on his life.

It is in this spot on the Adamello where John Paul's destiny, the meaning of his suffering, and his extraordinary life become ever more comprehensible, clear, almost luminous in spite of their tragic appearance. At that precise moment, in his eyes everything became acceptable, necessary, attributable to the will of God.

I

# ON THE TRAIL OF A SECRET

AND we saw in an immense light that is God: "something similar to how people appear in a mirror when they pass in front of it" a Bishop dressed in White "we had the impression that it was the Holy Father". Other Bishops, Priests, men and women Religious going up a steep mountain, at the top of which there was a big Cross of rough-hewn trunks as of a cork-tree with the bark; before reaching there the Holy Father passed through a big city half in ruins and half trembling with halting step, afflicted with pain and sorrow, he prayed for the souls of the corpses he met on his way; having reached the top of the mountain, on his knees at the foot of the big Cross he was killed by a group of soldiers who fired bullets and arrows at him, and in the same way there died one after another the other Bishops, Priests, men and women Religious, and various lay people of different ranks and positions. Beneath the two arms of the Cross there were two Angels each with a crystal aspersorium in his hand, in which they gathered up the blood of the Martyrs and with it sprinkled the souls that were making their way to God.

Tuy (Spain), January 3, 1944
The third secret of Fatima
Extract of the text of the message made public by the Church in 2000

Until a short time ago, I didn't know that fate had decided to bind my life to the profound meaning of these words made public by the Church such a long time after their original revelation. In my life, I had believed that I was playing a sort of game, in which things fell into place thanks to my efforts, to my work and my tenacity. I had satisfied most of my desires. Now I know that's not the way it is. Now I know that the days, hours, and minutes of my entire existence have unfolded according to a precise plan. I have simply been permitted to follow it. And this is what I have done.

My father, Martino Zani, class of 1931, was from the age of fifteen a "porter" on the ice of the towering Mount Adamello in the Italian Alps. As a porter he carried on his back, for skiers and tourists, food, drink, mountain equipment, and other gear, to the peak of more than ten thousand feet. He and his brothers, little more than children, took a long and difficult trail that started at the dropping off point of a cable car and wound its way upward, with stretches up sheer rock faces, passing along the Passo Brizio.

Every day, they faced an eight-hour walk to reach the Adamello shelter, a broad, low building constructed just after the end of the First World War. The shelter stood on what remained of an alpine barracks, which also included a little field hospital, right next to a magnificent view of the Lobbia Alta, a neighboring peak. The first approach went right by there: magnificent, scintillating views, and snow year round. But under that peaceful blanket of white, nature had hidden scenes of horrific catastrophe: thousands of dead Italian and Austro-Hungarian soldiers, who for the interminable years of the First World War had defended the ridges of those mountains.

It was a bloody war, called the "White War" precisely because it was fought in the midst of the perennial white snow. The Adamello is a mountainous mass that at its highest point reaches an elevation of 11,611 feet. There, until 1918, ran the border between Italy and Austria. It was this area that saw the advance of the Italian alpine units in 1915, to where the Garibaldi lodge stands.

The poor Italian soldiers resisted until, in 1918, the Austrians mounted an aggressive attack, aimed at breaking down the defensive line and cutting off the Italian advance beyond the Piave River. The front of Tonale-Adamello did not break, but the casualties were enormous. Those who did not die in combat then had to deal with the harshness of the three winters that followed. Survival became a tragic battle, in the perennial snow and in that hostile territory, swept by terrible winds and storms, with a temperature that, then as now, could fall to sixty degrees below zero. It was in that same place, about a dozen years after the end of the war, that the oldest summer ski resort in Italy was established by the Brescia chapter of the Club Alpino Italiano.

Also in 1935, my dad's father, Grandpa Melchiorre, had built a cabin using the leftover wood from the wartime barracks. It looked out over the Passo di Salarno, at an elevation of 10,000 feet, and was made of a double wall of wood and another of sheet metal, with a stove inside and a table that could seat six or eight persons.

In short, my family, originally from the village of Temù in the valley below, had earned its living for generations with "mountaineering" activities, renewing the covenant between the local population and the alpine summits, the majestic queens of that territory. We Zanis have belonged to this land for generations. Here we have dreamed, laughed, sung, drunk. Here we have fallen in love, we have suffered, lived, and buried our dead—always realizing, day after day, that we were engaged in a tacit and sometimes difficult covenant with nature. We Zanis have as our birthright an environment of superb beauty, but the mountains have never let us forget their boundless power.

In my earliest memory, there is a cone of shadow that plunges into the bowels of the earth, ready to swallow me up. Surprisingly, that danger instead resolved itself in a joyful leap, a jolt that tossed me into a "baptism of risk," as significant as a rite of initiation. It was the summer of 1961, I was just four years old, and for the first time my father took me to the top, to the lodge on the Adamello. We departed from an elevation of 8,300 feet, from the Garibaldi lodge, which my Mom and Dad were managing at the time. We walked for four hours without a break.

Without speaking, I climbed and struggled to keep up: my boots were brand-new, beautiful, but they rubbed against my heels, raising extremely painful blisters. It took a good bit of stubborn anger to keep going without saying anything, and evidently I had it. I climbed rock after rock, over level and broken ground, stony outcrops and bits of clearing, on a route that I would later in life come to know down to the last pebble.

At a certain point there was a crevasse, maybe a hundred and fifty feet deep, one of the kind that the July sun makes with ease. My father and the other adults could get across it with a quick hop. But no one felt like taking the leap with me in his arms: just a little uncertainty, some sudden movement by me, and we would end up at the bottom. So they tied a rope around my waist, secured it to the rock face with a carabiner, and pulled me over the precipice.

Looking back, I again see myself being whisked away like a leaf. I even feel the sudden fearful burst of saliva in my mouth, the fear mixed with a touch of mysterious euphoria. Again and again in my life I would taste it, fleetingly and always accompanied by an ephemeral, transitory happiness.

* * * * *

In 1969, my parents fulfilled a longstanding dream: to manage the lodge dedicated to the fallen soldiers of the Adamello (Trent). Here is a local news report from that time:

> In 1970, the first year of management under the Zani family, the work of modernizing the interior continues, thanks to the diligent work of the indefatigable Martino Zani. The wooden walls and floors are being redone, the gas and electric lighting system is being completed, the wooden floors are being painted, and all of the doors and windows are being replaced. A wooden terrace is being built to add to the outdoor space, very much appreciated for napping in the sun. Work has been done on the water lines, the interior restrooms, and the cable car. The Zanis have bought an electrical generator, refrigerator, washing machine, espresso machine, and a ski lift. After this work on the lodge, there is hot and cold running water, electricity, a snack bar, and fifty new beds. In the restrooms there are three sinks and a shower, and the kitchen has a big stainless steel sink, the boiler, refrigerator, and washing machine. Electricity is readily available for lighting and household use. The

> whole lodge has been redone from top to bottom, with new wooden floors in the common area and the lobby, new and freshly painted walls, renovated doors and windows. The furnishings are completed with the provision of fifty new cots, 100 sheets, and 120 blankets. "Humane" living conditions have been created for management, while the mountaineer can now find a hospitality and comfort there that are truly exceptional for those altitudes.
>
> Most of the credit for this undoubtedly belongs to the Zani family, which manages the lodge with intelligence and ability, a model of close collaboration and unity of purpose among the members of a nuclear family. In effect, the family is completely engaged in the management, each one having a role. From Grandpa Melchiorre, who waits patiently at the point of departure of the cable car in Bedole, to Martino's wife, Carla, a skilful director of everything and everyone, to Martino himself, an untiring worker always enthusiastic over new ideas and new efforts, to the three oldest children, all of whom share not only an interest in but a passion for the mountain and a devotion to the lodge.

So since the beginning of the 1960s, my family and I have always lived for five or six months, from spring to fall, at the lodge. There I was raised, like an animal in its habitat. My home was the glaciers, the rocks, the snow, roofed by the blinding sun that sets late and makes the days seem endless, as if they do not want to give in to the darkness, almost like a Nordic night.

There were four of us kids, two boys and two girls. I was the oldest, Franco was just a year younger than me, and then there were Renata and Miriam. Franco and I spent those years closer than twins, always together, as if one were the reflection of the other and neither had any substance on his own. Our parents worked in the lodge, and the two of us, from morning to evening, were the heroes of our solitary adventures. The ice was our playground: we climbed on it, shot at the rocks, skied tirelessly, blinded by the glare, at the limit of our strength, over treacherously broken ground, straining ourselves as if we were trying to dodge past a threat by heading straight at it, wild and free. Our favorite game was to go hunting for bombs dating back to the First World War, and blow them up. There were many of them in that area.

Those mountains were the site of what historians would later name the "Battle of the Glaciers." The passes of Lares and Cavento and the ridges of the Dosson of Genova-Cresta Croce and Monte Fumo were occupied by the Austrians in 1916. The mountaineers who were hoping to conquer these spots in their peaceful manner became aware that this would not be possible. There was terrible fighting, with enormous expense of ammunition, but also with the launching of bombs "spat out" by the Italians with a 149G cannon called "The Hippopotamus," which was hoisted up the Passo Venerocolo after many mishaps.

The responses came from another cannon, called "George," placed by the Austrians at the Mandrone shelter. The result: enormous casualties, so many that it is said that the expanses of snow were stained red by all the blood of those poor soldiers. And those who survived the battles still had to face the threat of death by exposure, and go to great lengths to survive under those conditions. In order to avoid or at least reduce to a minimum the possibility of such disasters, the army completed incredible projects like the digging of a tunnel almost three miles long, passing through the ice, and connecting the Passo Garibaldi with the Passo della Lobbia. Numerous barracks were built on the glaciers, connected to the valleys below with a vast network of cable cars. So a village arose around our lodge on the Adamello, a genuine citadel that was abandoned at the end of the conflict. In the story that I am telling here, the abandoned citadel is of great importance. Remember it.

We, the inhabitants of that enchanted place, saw the remains of that abandoned citadel rust and decompose over the years: iron, wood, explosives disabled by time and by the ice, as if nature had taken it upon itself to erase all that slaughter, all the outrage against life perpetrated in the soft underbelly of war. One day, as an adult, I would tell someone about this, unaware that I was talking about a scenario that—in the light of what I would come to understand later—must be brought to the attention of the entire world.

Returning to the carefree years of my childhood, I can say that, with the recklessness and flippancy of youth, Franco and I made these instruments of horror into our unusual playthings. The bombs attracted us with a fascination that was almost magnetic. The biggest of them weighed as much as 150 pounds. We secretly took them to a deserted spot, built a fire, and threw them in, making a sinister rumble that echoed all around the mountain peaks.

In the summer, when the remains of the barracks would reappear, the bitter odor of war would come back to our nostrils: the stench of rotten straw, the pungent smell of cordite and ballistite powder, the acid smell of iron eaten up by rust. Sometimes we would put the bombs near the lodge, as a terrible joke on the guests who were sleeping unawares. Around ten o'clock at night, we would set fire to little bundles of wood that we had placed all around the explosive, arranging them so that they would burn slowly. In the middle of the night: boom! Everyone awake, rushing out of the lodge in their pajamas. And us at our bedroom window watching and laughing with the coarse irreverence of that age.

When it came to punishment, my father was a little bit bark and a little bit bite. But he knew that it would do no good to stop us, he knew very well that for people like us, born in such singular environmental conditions, life and death play hide-and-seek practically every day. The crevasses that open all of a sudden, the insidious and unpredictable storms that are whipped up in a matter of minutes at high altitudes, the avalanches and all the rest constitute an environment that speaks of death, but teaches you about life.

Today I recall with a twinge of dismay that sometimes while we were playing there would be peeking out of the snow a skull, a shinbone, a thighbone . . . pitiful remains regurgitated by the glacier. There would be just a moment of surprise, and then we simply gathered them up, reciting under our breath, *Requiem aeternam dona eis Domine, et lux perpetua luceat eis. Amen.*

And then we were off and running to tell the grown-ups, who called the military chaplain of the Fourth Army Alpine Corps. He would come quickly by helicopter to perform his sacred duty. Placed in a casket, the remains were taken to a shrine that had been built on the Passo del Tonale. From time to time, a priest passing through would pause there to pray and give a quick blessing, and on certain special days there were ceremonies for the repose of those soldiers destined to remain unknown forever. Now I like to imagine that together with us, receiving those poor remains from our unintentionally disrespectful hands, was a host of angels. They were the ones, I am sure of it, who welcomed and watched over those poor soldiers killed in a ferocious but forgotten war.

The memory of so much suffering, the even more evident signs of that tragedy, the pity for all the men buried in a coffin of ice, were balanced by the rare beauty of those places. The lodge on the Adamello can be reached only on foot, after at least five hours of vigorous walking. There are three main access routes: from the Val di Genova, from the Passo del Tonale, and from the Garibaldi lodge below. Everywhere there is an identical landscape: deep green woods with larch trees, firs, and the imposing dwarf pine, a short and somewhat broad tree, from which a strong and restorative grappa was produced. Little by little, the most vigorous vegetation gives way to an acre of pasture, dotted in the summertime with the biggest and brightest stars that eye has ever seen. Continuing upward, the clear green gives way to brown, to the rocks peeking out of the retreating glacier, and then the splotches of rhododendron, although at that point moving through the area becomes difficult. It is there that the glacier begins, and the lodge suddenly appears, at first almost indistinguishable from the rock from which it is made, and then, as one gradually approaches, increasingly clear and austere in its rough simplicity.

At the lodge, a terrace looking out over the Lobbia like a balcony shows an endless expanse of glistening ice: this is the Pian di Neve. At first glance, the sight of that brilliant whiteness seems to take one's breath away. One feels like a weary, motionless dove, breathing in the peace: it is a good moment to rest the heart, sped up by the tough climb and by the thin atmosphere. One seems almost to absorb the reflection of all that brilliance. One feels intoxicated with a feeling of omnipotence, almost as if one could touch the sky. There are benches on that terraced lawn, and on that side, at sunset, the sunlight comes in slanted rays that tinge the perennial snows with pink, with a phantasmagorical effect. Little by little, looking down, one sees the cone of shadow that advances to swallow up the mountains. But that warm, gentle glow stays a long time, lapping against the night and bestowing the feeling of enjoying an absolute privilege, that of being in a little corner of paradise left standing on the earth. This is the spectacle that greets the visitor, the spectacle that found before it a "special being" who had arrived in this mountain area by what I erroneously believed, at that time, to be pure coincidence.

Every year in mid-March, at the beginning of spring, access is opened to the lodge dedicated to the fallen soldiers of the Adamello, and at that time, wherever in the world I may be wandering, I am seized as it were by a fever: to go back. In doing so, I am obeying a primitive code of belonging. I climb up, my heart beating harder and harder; I arrive almost exhausted, not so much from physical effort as from the emotion of returning to that womblike place which gathers me up in its unreal calm. That place—to the one who takes the trouble to pause there for a moment longer, finding the courage to delve within his own heart—cannot help but appear as a reflection of God. There is a voice that comes to the soul like a breath, and in a flash gives us a sign of its presence. This sign, for a brief but extremely intense moment, shows us the way to go at a particular moment in our lives—it is up to us to accept or reject it. Then it is as if one is stunned, with a slightly dazed smile on one's lips.

For a long, endless moment one remains in a daze, while everything seems to have stopped, reverent in the presence of something that is too great for us. Those who do not believe can speak of amazement before the majesty of the mountains and of nature. But I assure you, one senses the presence of something different, and even if for just a short time, one truly makes peace with oneself.

That lodge became little by little, over the years, the main activity of our family. We found it to be a bit worse for wear, deteriorated by the years and by the lack of painstaking care, which in such climatic conditions is necessary on an ongoing basis. We kids, together with Mom and Dad, dedicated ourselves completely to improving it, while preserving its original appearance. We worked hard, with great fervor and without feeling tired, as happens only with things that seem to belong to us and that stir up our love and enthusiasm.

Over the course of a dozen years or so, the skiing school built up quite a bit of business. There was always great demand during the summer months, and we sometimes had to accommodate more than 150 people at a time. Once Franco and I were of age, we became skiing instructors, while our mom and sisters looked after the lodge and its guests, and our dad supervised the shipping of supplies by cable car. I remember those years as the happiest of my life.

When the school that we attended in Temù let out for the summer, we kids literally escaped into the mountains, to the lodge, to stay there all summer. But every year the high point came at the moment in which, in the springtime, the gates opened for the beginning of a new season. The wooden entrance gate was protected by a robust and heavy bar of iron, and in the cold, dark lobby the air seemed stale, with a wintry heaviness that had to be driven out and dispersed in the fragrant air of the spring winds.

Making that big house breathe again, making the walls echo again with our laughter, our horseplay, our running up and down the stairs, all of this was a renewal of life, a resumption of purpose, a sense of the continuity of the places that warm the heart. The first things we kids did was to arm ourselves with hammers and go around pulling the nails out of the wooden shutters that were put over the windows when the lodge was closed, to prevent the powerful winter winds from doing irreparable damage when the temperature plummeted to twenty below zero.

Life at the Adamello lodge officially resumed when the chimney belched out its first puff of pungent smoke. It was the result of a lot of effort on Dad's part: he cleared the snow away from the flue and then lit the fire using newspaper and a fire striker, coughing and spitting. For two or three days, the house gave the impression of a huge bear slowly awakening from its hibernation, shaking its great frame, and freeing itself from the frost of winter. Thus the walls, the beams, the floors seemed to thaw to the heat of our voices, the fire, the life that was rekindling little by little.

Inside, the lodge looked like this: an entryway with an area for leaving boots; to the left a little snack bar where the guests who had just come in from the cold could have something hot to drink, and a door leading to the most lively and most visited part of the house. This was a large room illuminated by the natural light that came in through big arched windows. In that sitting room, dominated by a huge cast iron stove always full of wood, there were tables, chairs, and a few cupboards for storing plates and glasses. To the right was a big, well-furnished kitchen with a pantry behind it. A steep staircase led to the two upper floors, where there were eighteen bedrooms and a large dormitory with fifty-five beds, while others could be made up on the ground floor with sleeping bags or blankets.

Sleeping on the floor is normal under certain conditions, and besides, the mountaineers were not looking for creature comforts, and sometimes they arrived at the lodge unexpectedly in the evening, because they had fallen behind schedule or because the weather had taken a turn for the worse. Since there was no other shelter that could be reached without walking for several hours, we had to welcome everyone. I remember that on certain occasions, we accommodated two hundred persons in one night.

By the age of twenty, I had become what in our parts amounts to a fine "lad": a rebellious lock of blonde hair over my forehead, bright blue eyes, Dad's genetic gift to all of his children, the year-round tan of those who have the privilege of earning a living in such a place. During the summer, I worked along with the rest of my family on the activities of the lodge, and in the winter I worked with Franco at the skiing school that I had set up in Ponte di Legno. I had already understood that being a skiing instructor comes with a privilege, that of going straight to a woman's heart, and I definitely took advantage of this.

If the days had in store a vigorous pace up and down the slopes, the nights provided an activity just as intense, always conducted lightheartedly and with a touch of irony. All in all, it seemed to me that I was doing my gentlemanly duty in providing a service "included" in the tourist package . . . although my respect and sincerity were never lacking. Let's just say that my enchanting students were well aware that they simply wanted to enhance the joy of their vacation with a little extra dash of fun.

As a gentleman, I said nothing about who they were, and I promised myself that I would change my ways when I really fell in love. Besides, I was certainly not considered the "Casanova" of the family: my brother Franco was much more handsome and daring than I, and there was truly no counting his amorous conquests. He knew how to speak to a woman's heart, and he was always a man of great charm: with his bright blue eyes and dark hair, he was extremely popular as a skiing instructor and in the art of love. As for the Ganymede I was or believed myself to be, I was heading for a big letdown. I had fallen head over heels in love with Anna Rita, nicknamed "Iaia," a girl from Milan, beautiful, fascinating, and herself a lover of the mountains. She was a model, and for a while she seemed to go along with my propensity to lead an active and simple life, in contact with nature and immersed in my mountains. I wanted to marry her, and I had hastily built a beautiful home for us in Temù, my home town, which stands on a sunny plain of the Alta Val Camonica. I suddenly understood that it is precisely when you have planned your life in detail, when you have taken it for granted that what you want most is on the horizon, that the stroke of fate comes that smashes it all to pieces.

It is in these cases that one must begin to exercise patience, to discover an attitude that we human beings must never be without: that of knowing how to deal with adversity as serenely as possible. Iaia dumped me suddenly; she no longer loved mountain life and she no longer loved me, preferring to be with a man of more similar tastes and much older than her, who would become her husband. It was a tremendous blow, to which I reacted with fake nonchalance, telling her, “Let’s remain friends, don’t worry, I respect your decision,” while in reality I was going mad and suffering greatly, without showing it. At least my cure for that horrible pain was original: I decided to go to Alaska to climb Mount McKinley, at over 20,000 feet the highest mountain in all of North America. I remember the day, or rather the night, in which I decided to respond to my distress with that sudden departure. That memory is like a map of the heavens carved into the rock of my mountains: it was 1981, and my fate seemed to begin to enjoy itself in carrying me far away, as would happen again and again, and always with the lure of a new promise of life.

tastes and much older than her, who would become her husband. It was a tremendous blow, to which I reacted with false nonchalance, telling her, "I'll remain friends, but as ever I respect your choice," while in reality I was going mad and suffering greatly, without showing it. At least my cure for that terrible pain was original. I decided to go to Alaska to climb Mount McKinley, at over 20,000 feet the highest mountain in all of North America. I remember the day, or rather the night, in which I decided to respond to my distress with that sudden departure. That memory is like a thing of the heavens carved into the rock of my mountains: it was 1961, and my fate seemed to begin to express itself in carrying me far away, as would happen again and again, and always with the lure of a new promise of life.

II

# A GOOD "REFUGE" FOR THE POPE

A FEW years before my sudden departure, in Rome, more precisely at the Vatican, a certain event had drawn the attention and excitement of the whole world. On the evening of October 16, 1978, Karol Wojtyla was elected to the see of Peter, becoming Pope John Paul II, the pope from the East. I had followed the details of the exceptional event by spending a little more time than usual in front of the television, watching the evening news.

I still remember the moment I first saw his open, jovial face, that one-of-a-kind smile, the lively and luminous eyes that seemed that they might be laughing even more. I should have understood already from that smile who he would truly become, what he would represent for me, for us, for everyone, for history. But we human beings are always distracted and dazed by too much stimulation. So, I commented with a few inadvertent words, maybe like many others: "He seems nice, this pope!" Then my attention moved elsewhere—dinner, the telephone, talking with my parents, a review of the day. The superficial things that in the bustle of everyday life always seem more important than others, even when an alarm should ring to tell us that something is happening, and it has come to give meaning to our lives. The background of that memorable event would be recounted very well by a man who would later become very important in my life, to whom I would be bound, and still am, by a most profound affection. His name is Stanislaw Dziwisz. Today he is the archbishop of Krakow, and for thirty-nine years he was the pope's personal secretary. It was he who would later reveal that a moment before the attendants opened the curtains of the Hall of Blessings on the evening of that October 16, 1978, the pope murmured: "How will the Romans accept me, what will they say about a pope who has come from a faraway country?"

"He confided in me," Don Stanislao (as I call him) continued, "his preoccupation about Rome. He also told me that, as soon as he came to the window, he was reassured, because in the welcome of the people in Saint Peter's Square he had perceived a sentiment of hope. And that's exactly what he said, 'I felt the hope.'"

Don Stanislao was convinced immediately that between the Polish pope and Rome it was love at first sight. He also revealed that, as soon as he came back from the first blessing, he told the pope that the crowd had welcomed his election to the see of Peter with joy, and that he himself had personally touched that hope with his hand, seeing it in their faces, hearing it in the words of people in the crowd that had thronged into Saint Peter's Square.

Don Stanislao recounted another emblematic episode of the power of the pope's personality: "With a sheepish and somewhat humorous smile, he wanted to let me know about his first departure from protocol. Before the new pontiff appeared at the window, the master of ceremonies, Monsignor Virgilio Noè, had recommended that he impart the blessing in Latin without making any additional remarks. But John Paul II was unable to hold back, and started to speak in Italian. It was a greeting that remains historic: 'They have called me from a faraway country . . . if I make a mistake . . . if I make a mistake, you will correct me!'"

He also told us about what it was like for the pope right after the first blessing:

> He didn't get caught up in the craze. He wanted to have dinner with the cardinals, then he retired to the room that had been assigned to him for the conclave, on the mezzanine of the apartment of the secretary of state. He was sharing it with Cardinal Corrado Ursi. He sat down to write, in Latin, the introductory address for the Mass of the following day. And he began to think about the homily for the celebration of the beginning of his ministry. It is a

> homily that has remained famous for the motto, the guiding principle, of his pontificate: "Be not afraid! Open, rather, throw open wide the doors to Christ."

Then John Paul's secretary and longtime friend added that these words had ripened for him over the years. They were an expression of his faith. He had lived them, prayed them in private, and then expressed them with all of his ineffable spiritual power:

> The new successor of Peter in the see of Rome today makes a fervent, humble and trusting prayer: Christ, make me become and remain the servant of your unique power, the servant of your sweet power, the servant of your power that knows no eventide. Make me be a servant. Indeed, the servant of your servants.
>
> Brothers and sisters, do not be afraid to welcome Christ and accept his power. Help the pope and all those who wish to serve Christ and with Christ's power to serve the human person and the whole of mankind. Do not be afraid. Open wide the doors for Christ. To his saving power open the boundaries of states, economic and political systems, the vast fields of culture, civilization and development. Do not be afraid. Christ knows "what is in man." He alone knows it.
>
> So often today man does not know what is within him, in the depths of his mind and heart. So often he is uncertain about the meaning of his life on this earth. He is assailed by doubt, a doubt which turns into despair. We ask you therefore, we beg you with

> humility and trust, let Christ speak to man. He alone has words of life, yes, of eternal life.

The profound meaning of that message escaped me at that time—as I was only twenty-one years-old—just as it did millions of distracted Catholics in the rest of the world. They were extremely beautiful words, of course, but we considered them only words. Perhaps it was only later, with time, that we would realize that we were in the presence of the charisma of a future saint: a saint who would soon come, with simplicity, into my home and into my life.

* * * * *

Meanwhile, I learned to focus the restlessness of my twenties into excursions that at least a couple times a year brought me to scale various peaks of over 23,000 feet. I alternated between an essentially tranquil life, working as a skiing instructor on my mountains and living with my family, and trips that were truly full of challenge and emotion.

One of the first that comes to mind is an expedition I organized with three friends to scale the Ama Dablam, the sacred mountain of Nepal, almost 23,000 feet high. Together my little group of friends put together the ten million Lire (about $6,000) we needed for basic expenses, and set out enthusiastically. Nepal is a surprising country whose villages, during harvest season, take on the appearance of open-air granaries filled with mats on which the women spread grain to ripen in the sun. Ama Dablam truly has a special fascination: as soon as one arrives in the Khumbu valley, one looks at it in wonder and amazement. Its peaks are beautiful. It has elegant lines; perfect, as if drawn with the firm hand of an artist.

Starting to climb, we set a schedule of ten hours a day, and fortunately we had help carrying our roughly sixty pounds of equipment, food, and drink from the proud Sherpa, the descendants of the ancient caravaners who crossed the Nangpa La pass (elevation 19,049 feet), heading south with their yaks loaded with cargo. They are small people, but at the same time very strong, accustomed to truly prohibitive living conditions. For them, living most of life isolated between 10,000 and 15,000 feet in the Himalayan valleys, the sense of solidarity and of friendship is not just a manner of speaking. From Italy, we brought pasta, ham, Grana Padano, and energy bars.

Our porters cooked rice and the meat of wild goats, which they killed and set to boil with spices, making a savory stew. Deserving a special discussion of their own were the "untouchables" (a poor class of mountain people), who truly could not be approached. I remember that when one of them broke his leg, he didn't want us to take care of him. He preferred to be left there, alone, to wait for the assistance of his fellow untouchables, rather than violate the unbending rules imposed upon his caste.

In the valleys, the climate was typical of the jungle: suffocating heat, very high humidity, and the damned mosquitoes that were always swarming around our legs. But after a certain altitude, there were magnificent panoramas and breathtaking views. I still remember the women and children of the villages with their gentle smiles and their mixed expressions of curiosity and boldness. The young ladies did not fail to let us know that our Western faces and our features attracted them: they would suddenly stick out their tongues, as if to make an irreverent raspberry. I later learned that this was their way of saying, "I like you, I want to make love with you!"

I never took advantage of those offers, thinking an attitude of respectful friendliness would be better.

Back in Italy, however, I resumed my lifestyle of emotional disregard. I had fun. I was always surrounded by friends and girls, and I changed girlfriends frequently. But I was always very close to my family, and I never missed a birthday or any other family gathering—we were always a very united family, tightly knit in moments of both joy and suffering. In addition to my parents, I happily visited my aunts and uncles and cousins, those I could call members of a real and proper clan.

On May 13, 1981, I was driving with one of my aunts in my car. I was taking her back home, when we heard a truly dramatic news bulletin on the radio: in Saint Peter's Square, someone had shot the Holy Father, wounding him seriously. My aunt burst into tears, and I was stunned, not knowing how to console her or what to say. Who could want to hurt someone so universally loved?

A gloom hung over everyone in the days that followed. The pope was taken to the Gemelli hospital, where he was operated on for five and a half hours, while the whole world prayed that he would live, and the news media were constantly speculating on who else might have been behind the assassination by Mehmet Ali Agca. As soon as I returned home, I turned on the television and the radio to follow the news with apprehension. I was especially struck by the eyewitness account that the archbishop of Prague, Cardinal František Tomášek, gave on the radio:

> On the afternoon of May 13, the crowd, crammed into Saint Peter's Square, was joyfully waiting for the appearance of the Holy Father. Everything seemed normal. The sense of anticipation was becoming more intense, as demonstrated by a large group of young people who were chanting a greeting. The bells rang five, the signal that the moment longed for was near. All of a sudden, enthusiastic voices went up from the crowd: the Holy Father was coming, standing up in the jeep. He nodded in all directions, giving blessings, shaking countless hands, always with his fatherly smile on his lips. While he was handing back to her

smiling father a little girl who was beaming with joy at being held by the pope and receiving his blessing, suddenly something happened, like lightning out of a blue sky. A few shots were heard. The Polish priest Stanislao Dziwisz, the pope's personal secretary, and his valet, Angelo Gugel, grabbed the Holy Father by the arms as he collapsed, his white cassock turning red with blood. It is impossible to describe the general distress: one had to see it.

The pope's jeep sped off toward the front of the basilica, where a few ambulances are always ready during the audiences. John Paul II was loaded onto one of them, which immediately headed off to the Policlinico Agostino Gemelli. None of those present were able to hold back their tears, one heard sobbing, but above all there was prayer: prayer gives light and strength at the most difficult times. At six o'clock, the Holy Father was already on the operating table; he had lost so much blood that he needed a transfusion of six pints. There was a serious gunshot wound in his chest, and two less serious ones in his right shoulder and on the index finger of his right hand, but no vital organ had been injured. The surgery ended at about 11:30, and the Holy Father was moved to the intensive care unit.

On Thursday, Friday, and Saturday, Holy Mass was celebrated in his room and the pope received communion; he drew great inner peace from constant prayer. By Sunday, he was already able to concelebrate the Mass, seated in his bed, along with two personal secretaries. He continued his apostolic work, united

> with Christ through prayer and accepting suffering beside the Virgin Mary: with this attitude, he strove to realize better and better the motto *Totus Tuus*.
>
> The cynical assassin, twenty-three-year-old Mehmet Ali Agca of Turkey, tried to escape after the attempt, but was arrested and taken away by the police. Interpol has a file on him: two years ago, Agca made a death threat against the pope when he was visiting Turkey; in Rome, he had taken a hotel room near the Vatican and from there had made several international telephone calls. The police found a considerable sum of money on his person: his frequent trips through Europe, his contacts and the large amount of money he possessed without working, demonstrate that his activity was intended and planned.
>
> In addition to the Holy Father, two women who were near him were injured, one of them, an American, very seriously. It is a distressing fact that in our society, which prides itself on belonging to an age of high cultural and technological development, there should exist such a "jungle": this is a moral cancer that must be dug out at the roots. The Holy Father sees his attacker as a poor misled man, and forgives him from his heart.

Our religious devotion as a family was always marked by simplicity, a solid faith without uncertainty, without crises, but that emphasized doing our duty toward our relatives and others over the strict observation of precepts. In the winter, everyone went to Mass at the little church of Temù. In the summer, we said a prayer together in the morning, usually because Mom wanted us to, and . . . Amen.

But the Lord has always been present in my life: two times I have been on the verge of crossing the threshold between life and death, and two times I came back, because that's what had been decided up there. For me, God's "brushstrokes" were in nature: in the pink light that tinted the glacier at sunset, in the magenta of the lichens peeking out from between the rocks, in the vibrant fuchsia of the rhododendrons or in the perfection of the dappled coats of the fawns.

* * * * *

During the months we spent at the lodge, we attended Mass only when a priest came up, and we would ask him to celebrate it. And since priests came through fairly often, it seemed perfectly normal to us when four Polish priests arrived one afternoon in the middle of June in 1984. I remember everything perfectly, like the scenes in a movie: it was in the afternoon, and I was coming back from the cable car, about half a mile from the lodge, where I had loaded some food provisions.

I found them in front of me all of a sudden, standing in the front yard near the benches, engrossed in their conversation. They had hiked for several hours up through the beautiful green Val di Genova, accompanied by Gianluca Rosa, a skiing instructor and a childhood friend of mine, who gave us a hand with skiing lessons in the summer. In the evening, I joined them for a chat in the dining room.

I was immediately struck by the manner of speaking of the one who spoke the best Italian, Don Stanislao. He must have been about forty-five, with the round, good-natured face of an easygoing rural priest. But his eyes did not give the impression of someone slow of mind, being rather the spies of an absolutely superior spirit of observation and capacity of comprehension. His eyes bored attentively into you. They were not devoid of empathy and kindness, but they could delve right into your soul and perfectly grasp your feelings. At the time, I could not have known that everyone considered him a man of great heart. He had been the person closest to the pope since 1966, when he had become chaplain to Cardinal Wojtyla in Krakow.

I could not have known then that he had always been close to the Holy Father, clasping the wounded man in his arms on that terrible afternoon of May 13, three years before. I did not know that his relationship with the pope was more like that of a son with his father than that of an employee with his boss.

Another of them, Father Tadeusz Styczen, whose name I always Italianized as Taddeo, was also very close to the Holy Father: first as his student, then as his successor as ethics professor at the Catholic University of Lublin, and always with him at times of recreation. That evening, we were seated at the same table for dinner. For them as for everyone else, we served a good hot soup, cold cuts, cheese, eggs, and a nice slice of pie. As the only privilege we uncorked a bottle of excellent vintage red wine, but that was more for my friend Gianluca than out of deference for the four Polish priests. After dinner, we played cards.

And, thanks to a shot of grappa and the family atmosphere that only the camaraderie of a mountain lodge can create, in no time at all we were joking together like old friends. I even accused Don Stanislao of cheating, and after pretending to get mad he laughed until tears came down. Chatting amiably, Don Stanislao told me that he, Father Taddeo, and the other two would like to get up early the next morning and go skiing. And that in order to do this, they would need to borrow some equipment, since they had none with them.

We solved the problem with no difficulty, finding each of them skis, boots, and the rest. And the next morning, around eight o'clock, after a big breakfast, we were out on the slopes. Overnight there had been a violent storm, with thunder, lightning, and a lot of snow. Then suddenly the weather had turned fair, putting a shine on the colors as if that place was the theater for an important and carefully crafted performance.

We went skiing on the Lares glacier, which stood

of 11,000 feet and dropped down into a beautiful valley that declined to 9,000 feet. The sun was high in the sky, the snow was compact and sparkling, and the mountains were full of the grandeur of creation that God has so generously bestowed on them. At a certain point, they asked to go for a ride around the surrounding area in the snowcat that my father used to bring clients back to the summit, since there was no ski life there.

Around noon, we came back to the lodge. Before he left, Don Stanislao went to the kitchen to talk to my mother, Carla: "Mrs. Carla, I am the personal secretary of the Holy Father. What would you say if I were to bring him here?" To this day, my mother swears she thought he was delusional, but her kindly nature nonetheless led her to agree to the proposal: "Father, do you have to ask? It would be the most wonderful thing that ever happened to me!"

Afterward, she pulled me and Franco aside to tell us about the crazy thing the priest had just asked her. At that point, Don Stanislao came back over and began to talk with me about that extraordinary possibility. He advised me that absolute secrecy would be necessary, or the pope's vacation could not take place. Then, Mom and I took Don Stanislao on a tour of the whole lodge. We showed him the tiny bedrooms with their spartan furnishings, just a cot, a chair, and a clothes rack. We told him that there were only two bathrooms on each floor, which would have to be enough for everyone.

Mom was worried, and asked, "But Father, what should we do, what should we change?"

With a friendly smile, he replied, "Mrs. Carla, you don't have to change a thing, it's all fine as it is."

III

# TWO FRIENDS ON THE SNOW: THE POPE AND PERTINI

AFTER those unusual guests departed, Mom, Franco, and I sat down to talk with a mixture of disbelief and concern about the strange and completely unexpected possibility that John Paul II could be eating, sleeping, and praying at our lodge in the middle of nowhere. We decided to face the matter rationally, thinking above all of maintaining the absolute requirement of secrecy. We decided to keep the matter a secret among ourselves, not even telling Dad or the rest of the family. But we came to the conclusion that we would at least have to tell Miriam, my younger sister, who was living in Temù, at our house in the valley north of Adamello. We thought her help would be indispensable, because at the time there was no telephone service at the lodge. It had only a two-way radio connection with Bedole, where the cable car my father managed was located. Using this, we could call Miriam in Temù and the barracks of the carabinieri in Pinzolo to the East (in the province of Trent) for any emergency communications.

So Mom, Franco, Miriam, and I became partners in the feverish work of preparation. We had arranged with Don Stanislao that the pope would stay with us on July 16, 17, and 18, giving us exactly one month to get ready.

I have often wondered over the years why Don Stanislao chose our lodge and the glacier of the Adamello for a vacation for the Holy Father. I think it was because of the uniqueness and beauty of that place, and also because of the understanding that we Zanis were good Christians and "mountaineers" of few words, and therefore capable of keeping a secret.

During our first encounter, Don Stanislao did not ask me any questions about the battles of the First World War on the Adamello, much less about Cresta Croce and the little wooden cross erected at the summit of that mountain in memory of the many soldiers who died. I emphasize this apparently irrelevant detail to make it clear how back then we were all totally unaware of the true significance of what was about to happen.

There was something of great value here, belonging to the realm of the transcendent, but hidden in the most disarming simplicity of a vacation. It would still take many years, until the glorious day of beatification was near, for me and others finally to understand, feel, and accept what today appears plausible to logic and undeniable to faith. At the time it seemed that fate and fate alone was responsible for the arrival of that man dressed in white.

As soon as Don Stanislao and the others had left, we decided not to take any more reservations for the days during which the pope would be there. As for the few people already scheduled to be there, we were told not to cancel their reservations. The following day, after a night disturbed by a thousand doubts, I went to town on foot and with great reservation spoke to my sister about what had happened, telling her about all of my concerns.

"Let's call the Vatican directly, and we'll find out if all of this is true and will happen as explained to you," she suggested.

We did so, and not only was everything confirmed, but we were informed that we would soon receive a visit from a Commander Camillo Cibin. Only later did I learn that Cibin was an institution in Vatican circles. He was John Paul II's guardian angel for many years, the person who followed him everywhere and provided for his security. There are photos of Cibin on the day of the attack in Saint Peter's Square that have been seen all over the world. After the shots were fired he leaped over the security barrier to stop Ali Agca from getting away. The next year, Cibin had the quick reflexes to grab the arm of another madman armed with a knife, who wanted to kill the pope during his visit to Fatima.

Cibin arrived at our lodge by helicopter about ten days after our call to the Vatican, around the first of July.

Mom, who thought it was an inspection by the national health service, burst into the room and was simply told, "Ma'am, if everything is okay the pope is coming to stay with you!"

At the height of the confusion, Mom sent for me. I interrupted the skiing lesson that I was giving and in a few minutes I was back down at the lodge.

Holding her hand, I observed: in front of her was a distinguished man of straightforward and abrupt manners, very sure of himself and energetic. Over the years I would come to learn that behind that coldness was a generous soul. I would come to understand his preoccupation in evaluating all the aspects of the security detail. I even came to admire the slightly crafty smile that lit up his face when it was just us, people on the inside, close to the Holy Father.

After surveying the surroundings, Cibin wanted to inspect every corner of the lodge, and asked to see the room that we were thinking of offering to the pope. We had chosen one at the end of the hallway on the second floor, like all of the others, meaning it didn't even have a private bathroom. But he told us that it would be just fine, advising us to add a kneeler, a small nightstand, and a simple chair.

There was a bunk bed with three berths: we took this apart, leaving only a folding bed, and Mom put a wooden crucifix on the bare wall in front of the bed. Right next door, as we had been asked, we set up a nearly identical room for Don Stanislao. Cibin then asked what we would be making to eat, and we arranged this with him as well, choosing a simple—but abundant and genuine—menu. Mom made the selections: local cured meats, gnocchi made with bread and wild spinach, alpine cheese, wild berries, fruitcake, all washed down with white Tocai wine and local grappa.

The most absolute secrecy was maintained both by us and by the few members of the pope's inner circle who knew about this extremely private visit to the Adamello. But three days before his departure, on July 13, something unexpected happened that made the event even more exceptional, prompting the curiosity and amusement of the whole world. For his travels, the Holy Father had to use the means provided for him by the Italian air force. So a request was sent to the government for authorization for a flight from Rome to Verona, and then for a helicopter from Verona to the Adamello. Someone, apparently an air force colonel, told the news to one of his friends on the staff of Italian president Sandro Pertini.

At that point, Antonio Maccanico, the secretary general of the Quirinale (the president's residence), learned about it and spoke directly with the president, having been his close confidant since Pertini was president of the Chamber of Deputies.

Maccanico said to Pertini, "Who knows where the pope has to go in such great secrecy?"

A few years later, Don Stanislao himself told me the

highly amusing scene that unfolded, and in the same way I'm about to tell it now. Since the pope and the president were good friends, and no official event or visit was scheduled, the straightforward and beloved president picked up the phone: "Now I'll just ask my friend Karol where he intends to go!"

Like a kid who gets caught playing a prank, the pope chuckled and quickly replied, "I'm going skiing, on a trip to the magnificent glacier of the Adamello. Why don't you come too, President?"

And Pertini: "Okay, Holy Father, let's go!"

The results of that conversation would bring the two of them up to us in a matter of a few hours. That same afternoon, in fact, Cibin came back by helicopter together with the police chief and vice-prefect of Trent, who, with an evidently greater sense of urgency, began to inspect the surrounding area from top to bottom. After painstaking inspection, they met with me in the lodge to let me know about their decisions.

They had told the local authorities that the area would have to be cleared of munitions left over from the war, and access would be tightly controlled. The area was made off-limits on July 15, and Italian state security officers asked us to remove the few persons who were staying at the lodge. So we sent them away, a family of five and two men, the persons whom Don Stanislao had told us could stay. We lied to them and said that because bombs were being cleared out they were in great and imminent danger. Two helicopters came and took them away in great haste.

Mom became even more agitated when she was told that President Pertini was a vegetarian. She went into damage control, adding to the menu a risotto, an Olivier salad, vegetables au gratin, and other various kinds of salads. On that same day, the eve of the great event, Don Stanislao, Cibin, and Father Taddeo came up on foot and stayed the night to make sure that everything was in place. After dinner, I took Don Stanislao aside and started to pepper him with questions: "How should I greet him? Should I kiss his ring or not? Should I call him 'Your Holiness' or 'Holy Father'?"

He smiled and shook his head: "Come on, Lino, do what comes naturally, don't create problems for yourself, welcome him as you would welcome a friend!"

Easy for him to say! Imagine that tomorrow the pope is going to be sitting on your couch, having dinner with you, and sleeping at your house.

That night I slept very little if I slept at all, and I was already up and around at four o'clock in the morning. It was a wonderful day. At 8:45 we began to hear the sound from the rotors of a big military helicopter, the kind that can hold up to twelve people. It landed in a clearing on the Passo della Lobbia, about five hundred feet from the lodge. The welcoming party was extremely small: just me, my brother Franco, Dad, my sister Renata and her husband, the girls who helped Mom serve meals, and the son of some friends, nine-year-old Enrico, whom we had told to come for a surprise without giving away anything more.

When the door was opened, the first to come out was the Holy Father, wearing a black cloak over his white cassock. I will never forget the look on his face: a bit of deeply ingrained irony, a lively curiosity, and something like the ability to caress you with his eyes. I felt like I was being soothed by a love made available to all, from which anyone could benefit by simply looking at it, regardless of merit. When I think back on it today, I realize that this was the first sign of "holiness" that I witnessed, feeling myself invaded by a subtle and penetrating sensation, a combination of lightheartedness and joy. I was just twenty-seven and had a wonderful and adventurous life, but if I had been old and sick, or weighed down with some sort of suffering, I am sure that simply seeing him would have alleviated the pain. My brother Franco and I approached him right away, and I bent down slightly to kiss his ring. The pope immediately pulled me back up, and then I heard the slow cadence of his voice, with a slight and unmistakable drawl: "What is your name?" And then: "So, today we're going skiing together. . . ."

This was another characteristic of his: the capacity to understand immediately who was in front of him, and why. Just by looking at me he had understood that I, and no one else, would be his skiing instructor, or rather his guide, since he was already good at skiing. In spite of the injuries he had suffered, John Paul II looked like he was in good shape, and so I immediately went to help Pertini hop down from the helicopter. I used the term "hop" for the president, and it's not a mistake, because the impression that he gave, although he was in his eighties, was that of a "live wire" jumping around and talking nonstop. We had to walk a few hundred feet to the snowcat, which my dad would drive to the lodge.

But we had to walk on the ice, and I was immediately concerned about the safety of the four or five men of the president's staff. Anyone who had seen them from a distance would have burst out laughing: they were wearing jackets and ties and walking on the crusted snow in leather shoes. Evidently, because of the iron-clad rule of secrecy, no one had told them about the unusual destination of that odd couple. They were sliding all over the place. It was truly comical. But the president was outfitted perfectly: calf-length trousers tucked into excellent brown boots with Vibram soles, a Nordic-pattern sweater, and his ever-present cane. The scene that followed was truly exhilarating.

After boarding the snowcat and riding a short distance, we came to a trail leading to the entrance to the lodge. It was rocky, broken, and unstable due to the nature of the terrain. My brother and I grabbed the arms of the president, who was clearly having trouble. And he began to complain with his usual vehemence: "But what kind of trail is this? We can't have the Holy Father walking here, you should have told me about it, I would have taken care of it, I would have sent a mountaineer corps up here and they could have leveled it. What are we going to do now?"

I looked at John Paul II, who was walking a few steps ahead of us. He was walking alone, peacefully, just barely leaning on the arm of Gigi, a security agent walking next to him. I saw him shaking his head and smiling in amusement, like a child smiles at the usual tantrums of an incorrigible friend. Franco and I arrived at the lodge holding the president by the arms, not even letting his feet touch the ground, while he continued protesting vigorously, concerned about His Holiness.

My mother and sisters were waiting for us at the entrance to the lodge. Mom greeted the pope at the door. He came in, smiled at her, and stopped her from stooping down to kiss his hand. Instead he took both of hers in his and held them tight, responding to her few words of greeting with an exquisite smile. To this day, Mom says the contact with his hands brought her a sensation she had never felt before or since in her life. It was a sort of warmth that brought well-being, a jolt of beneficial energy, which went beyond the emotion of seeing such an important person.

I must say that after this, the pope demonstrated a great bond of affection with Mamma Carla. Over the years he always took great interest in her health and dedicated special thoughts and prayers to her. Moreover, the pope had lost his beloved mother, Emilia, at just nine years of age. It is normal to forge a bond of affection with a woman as tough and yet kind as my mother, who probably reminded him of his own. It was Mom who prepared with her own hands a nice, hot, foamy cappuccino to warm him up as soon as he arrived. He accepted it with enthusiasm, but again he had to put up with the objections of Pertini: "What's this with the cappuccino, Your Holiness? We're mountain men here, look at me, I'm going to drink a nice little grappa, not a cappuccino. . . . Me, I'm a mountaineer, and mountaineers don't drink cappuccino . . ."

Indeed, there was much laughter and good humor. Immediately after drinking his cappuccino, the Holy Father asked to go upstairs to change. He was truly anxious to get the skis on his feet. After just a few minutes, he came down from his room a perfect and simple skier: blue pants and windbreaker, gloves of the same color, a white cap with a brim, sunglasses and a pair of cheery red boots, which added a truly elegant touch to his sportsman's outfit. Pertini had his ever-present pipe in his hand, and in great excitement said over and over again, looking out the window of the sitting room: "What a place, what a delight, what a magnificent day!"

It was he who began to speak first about the Great War, evoking the scenes, the sacrifices of the mountaineers, the resistance not only against the enemy but against the cold, the prohibitive environmental conditions, and the lack of food and provisions. I remember that he talked for a long time about the "forgotten war," about poor Christs abandoned by those in command.

Pertini continued to talk about the war after we had boarded the snowcat to ride to the Lares glacier slope. Behind, in the open-air seats, were me, my brother Franco, the president, and his personal physician. There were also Antonio Maccanico in jacket and tie, the pope's bodyguard, and Angelo Gugel, valet to the Holy Father. Gugel wanted to sit in the cabin next to Dad, who was driving. I would later learn that during that half-hour, my father took advantage of the situation to "use" that very special "shepherd of souls," asking him to hear his confession.

A few minutes after nine, we were already on the white expanse of snow, excellent and compact cover on that truly idyllic day in terms of the weather. We put our skis on at the Lares glacier slope. At first I tried to stay close to the pope, but then I realized that he was doing perfectly fine without my help, and in fact preferred to be on his own. We made run after run, going up in the "cat" and skiing back down. I always went before the pope, for two reasons. First, Don Stanislao wanted some photos, and since there was no photographer present, he asked me to take some. Also, I always wanted to be the trail-blazer for safety reasons. In fact, I had explained to the Holy Father that the insidious danger of those perennial and marvelous snows was that there were countless crevasses. So I asked him to take the same path down the slope that I had taken.

Other than that, the pope skied very well, confidently, with his skis parallel like an expert skier. He was even a bit of a daredevil. He loved the slope, the steepest runs. He had an unusual and unique posture, leaning forward a bit, but this was probably due to the fact that when he had learned to ski in the Tatra Mountains in Poland, where the skis were more rigid and required that kind of posture.

He was imaginative in selecting the runs, asking me if we could start from one spot rather than another. There was a light, fleeting happiness that flashed across his face during the speedy descent, and his eyes became those of a child, carefree and profoundly joyful. Every now and then he would exclaim, "Lino, what exceptional snow you have up here!" The snowcat, with Pertini and the other guests on board, accompanied us and then descended to the valley, waiting to take us back up until the president, with his booming voice, called out to the pope, "Your Holiness, you ski like a swallow!":

Around noon—we were right at the Passo del Lares, the highest pass of the Adamello—the pope suddenly stopped to recite the Angelus. It was an endearing habit in which I would learn to participate, something that marked the rhythm of his life, repeated invariably in the morning, at noon, and at sunset. We would go to a corner and he would begin with his firm voice in the silence:

"The angel of the Lord declared unto Mary . . ."

The prayer was as brief as a breath, and then we resumed skiing for a few minutes. Immediately afterward, something happened that I will never forget, and that let me intuit, although still in a confused manner, how the universe was truly beginning to make me understand the story of the Other. A slender thread had begun to unwind in that long-ago May of 1917, starting from the gloomy setting of the war, and wrapping around events in different years and different places in the world: Fatima, the Adamello, Rome, and Saint Peter's Square.

Only as I write this, on the eve of John Paul's beatification, a day of glory, does that thread appear to me in every one of its details . . . utterly clear.

IV

# THE SILENCE OF PRAYER

AS WE made our descent, we ended up near a slope that started from the stubby remains of a tower built as an observation point during the war, and ended near a rock wall up against the one called the Punta Attilio Calvi. We local mountaineers simply called the area "road of the alpines." His curiosity piqued, the pope asked me who that Attilio Calvi was, and since I knew the story at least in part, I started to tell him about the Calvi brothers, that unfortunate and heroic family.

The four Calvi brothers, Attilio, Santino, Natale, and Giannino, were born in Piazza Brembana in the province of Bergamo. Their father, Gerolamo Calvi, was the mayor of the town, and their mother, Orsolina Pizzigoni, was a religious, intelligent, and courageous woman. The brothers all died young after fighting for their country in the Great War and became heroes. They were noble, romantic, and combative, and distinguished themselves in battle, earning fifteen medals of military valor.

Attilio was born on November 4, 1889, and obtained a law degree, but did not practice as a lawyer, because at the age of twenty-two he went off to the war in Libya. After this, he enlisted in the 51st company of the alpine battalion "Edolo," and won his first medal for military valor for his calm and courage. He was very familiar with our mountains, an expert mountaineer and a member of a group of rock climbers. In 1915, at the outbreak of the First World War, he was made a second lieutenant of the battalion. His first engagements were in Montozzo, in the mountains between the Adamello and the Tonale. Here he distinguished himself for courageous military operations like that of August 21, 1915, an expedition aimed at the conquest of Punta Albiolo, which removed an important Austrian stronghold. This success won him his second bronze medal.

On September 25, he led the conquest of the tower of Albiolo. With only four men and under enemy fire from about ten yards away, Attilio led the decisive assault with his legendary composure. He was awarded a silver medal. In April of 1916, he was pushed to the limit in the terrible battle aimed at driving the Austrians into retreat from the area around the Dosson di Genova, the very region of the Adamello. These were terrible days. There were low clouds and the snow fell copiously on the glacier, that rose over ten thousand feet. Many of the soldiers were mortally wounded, including Attilio, who passed away after two days of agony. And this was how the name was given to the peak, at an elevation of 10,797 feet, over which I was gliding along with the pope.

The same evil fate befell his brother Santino, who on May 29, 1915, just five days after the beginning of the war, won his first silver medal for acts of valor on the Vezzena peak. He had left his trench three times, braving enemy fire, to carry to safety three fellow soldiers who had been wounded by the Austrians. Then, one cold December night he was shot in the face, the bullet fracturing his jaw. After unspeakable suffering, he resumed fighting while still recovering from the injury and won another bronze medal. In the summer of 1917, he was given another extremely dangerous mission: the conquest of the Passo dell'Agnello, the highest pass in the Alps. Fully aware of the risk and perhaps in the grip of an ugly premonition, he sent his mother a goodbye letter. Then he told his men, "You will see, today, how an officer of the Italian alpine corps dies." It was June 10, and after taking an important position he was shot in the shoulder, while another bullet grazed his forehead. In spite of this, he continued to fight and to urge his men on, until another bullet went through his heart. He died saying, "This time they got me."

Giannino was the youngest of the four, and he did not want to become a soldier, but rather a priest. But after Attilio and Santino died, he changed his mind and decided to go off to the war. He refused to be exempted from fighting on the front line, saying that he wanted to honor the memory of his fallen brothers by fighting generously himself. He was assigned to the machine gun corps, where his captain was his brother Natalino, beside whom he fought with great courage. Giannino was never wounded.

As fate would have it, as he was returning home after the war, he fell victim to the Spanish flu which took his life after a brief but agonizing ordeal. He died before he was able to see his family again. A cross was later set up in his memory.

The last remaining brother was Natalino. After various episodes of true heroism and military conquest, he was seriously injured in 1918. It was the final year of the war, and he was in command of the Monte Suello battalion. His injuries left him with a mutilated foot. The only survivor of the four at the end of the war, he returned home, but could find no peace. The tremendous alpine battles, the sufferings he had endured, the deaths of his brothers had deeply scarred him. The hero of the Cavento (the mountain in the Adamello where he led his men to victory), as everyone called him, was now living in his own world, often absorbed in it or completely gone, seemingly unable to return to everyday life. On September 16, 1920, he tried to climb a rock face with a thousand-meter drop. Perhaps he was challenging himself, or even death. He left from the Garibaldi lodge to the southern face of the Adamello, but about halfway up he was caught in an avalanche.

He fell into the void and was smashed against the rocks below.

His father, burdened by the drama of the death of all four of his sons, died of a broken heart shortly after the end of the war, leaving only his wife. She was renamed "Mamma Calvi," and became a point of reference to honor the memory of her sons and tell about their legendary deeds. King Vittorio Emanuele III, Mussolini, and Gabriele d'Annunzio gave public tribute to the Calvi, and d'Annunzio even erected a monument in Piazza Brembana. The plaque reads:

> Natale, Attilio, Sante, Giannino.
> Flower of Italy's youth,
> pride of their native Piazza Brembana.
> The four Calvi brothers,
> with the power of an eagle,
> defended in war the mountain peaks of their fatherland.
> Death extinguished them,
> glory crowned them with the immortal laurel.

Even today, the Mamma Calvi Foundation bestows awards on Italy's most outstanding students on November 4, the anniversary of the end of the war.

I told the pope that Attilio had died right behind that rock face that we were standing near. I pointed out that the wooden ladders nailed into the granite had been put there by the alpine soldiers all those years ago. I explained to him that the front had run along that precise spot on the mountain: the Italians on this side, the Austrians on that side, and since not all the alpine soldiers were climbers, they needed the ladders to get up to the summit to fight.

I still remember exactly the expression on the pope's face. He was thoughtful for a moment, then he mentioned the stories of the First World War that his father Józef, who had fought in it, had told him when he was a child. He added that many young Poles, especially from his home, Krakow, had fought for the Austrian army and had died there.

* * * * *

Further down, we saw the remains of the barracks that made up that citadel of the mountaineer corps, and he wanted to stop again for a moment to pray for those souls, for all those soldiers who had lost their lives. We had planned to keep skiing for another hour, before returning to the lodge for lunch. Suddenly, however, the Holy Father seemed to change his mind. His expression was completely different, the smile gone from his eyes and his face. He and Don Stanislao had a brief conversation in Polish. Many times during the twenty-one years in which I had the good fortune to spend time with the pope, I would witness such moments characterized by a fast-paced dialogue, intimate and a bit mysterious, conducted quietly in Polish so that no one would understand.

The bond between them was very strong, and it was clear that they understood each other with just a look. Don Stanislao approached me and whispered, "Lino, the Holy Father wants to be alone for a little while in recollection, let's look for a good spot."

The others who were skiing with us moved a short distance away, while Don Stanislao and I looked around for just the right little nook. We spotted it nearby, a big flat rock that curiously looked like a sort of couch with one armrest. The pope was standing with his elbow propped against his chest and his head resting on his hand. That outcrop of the Passo di Lares was positioned exquisitely, looking out over all of the Val Rendena, the Brenta mountain group, the Monte Bondone, almost to the city Trento—from there the gaze could roam almost to infinity. I remember that a special atmospheric phenomenon of our locale could be seen in the cobalt-blue sky: on particularly sunny days, a sort of haze forms in the valley, blurring the boundary between earth and sky and melting everything into one.

Then Don Stanislao said, "Lino, you go with him!"

I took him by the hand and helped him to sit down, and then I respectfully took a few steps back, as did all the others. It was then that I witnessed for the first time something I will truly never forget, and that—overcoming my reservations—I am telling here for the first time. I seek to do so accurately and with purity of heart.

His head was bowed and he was absorbed in prayer, totally immobile, without even the slightest movement. He was in a sort of trance—or I dare say, ecstasy—which he was modestly hiding from us. In fact, I couldn't see his face or even tell whether his hands were folded or not. Nor if his eyes were open or closed. Instead, I had the very clear sensation that I was observing someone endowed with a spiritual power that was no longer human; someone who no longer belonged to this world, but was living those minutes in complete communion with God, with the saints, and with all the souls of heaven.

The unreal sparkle of the snow all around emphasized this impression. A complete silence had descended. Everything was motionless, as if a state of contemplation had taken hold of every element of nature.

There was no flapping of a wing or the call of a bird, no gentle impact of clumps of snow falling to the ground, no squeak of boots moving over the glacier. Everyone—and everything—seemed to be under a spell that had taken away the power of speech and movement, as if we were in a children's fairy tale. I know that setting so well—the peaks, the glaciers. I have spent much of my life in places like that, and I know that the silence of the mountain is full of voices, sounds, animal cries, the wind itself.

At that moment, however, everything seemed to have stopped, truly everything. As if under a spell. There were a number of us there, and everyone could confirm this sensation. I can say with complete conviction that I touched with my hands, just like Saint Thomas. I saw how a normal man can cross the boundary and emanate sanctity. A stone and the bare rock certainly do not make for a soft couch, and yet he did not tire. He never moved so much as a millimeter, his muscles were motionless like everything else around him. Then, the strangest thing occurred. The pope, after tiniest imperceptible movement, revived and then slowly got up, and when we looked at our watches, realized that almost an hour had gone by.

Don Stanislao spoke again: "Go, Lino, help him."

I went to get him. The normal flow of things and time resumed, and we put our skis back onto our feet. But a strange silence remained—no one had the courage to speak, and everyone had a slightly dazed expression because of what we had just witnessed. But none of us spoke of it—at that time or afterward—as if we had been in the presence of something extremely mysterious and yet absolutely simple. Lower down in the valley, however, where he was waiting for us, President Pertini started protesting vigorously: "Why are you so late? You had us worried!" We then returned to the lodge for lunch. Standing, John Paul II recited together with all of us, "Bless, O Lord, this food that you have given us in your goodness. Provide also for those who have nothing, and make us participants in your blessing. Through Christ our Lord. Amen."

Then we all sat down at the table. I was sitting across from the pope, Pertini was sitting at his right, and Don Stanislao at his left. I remember that when my sisters were serving the spinach gnocchi, which were called "strozzapreti" ("priest-chokers") where we lived, Pertini made a quip that later became famous: "Sorry, Your Holiness, but today we're going to do you in!"

Pertini's personal physician was sitting next to him, and the two of them put on quite the show for us. At every course, the president would ask, "May I have just a little bit more, may I have seconds?"

And his physician: "But, Mr. President . . ."

And he: "Doctor, think about your own plate, look at your plate, not mine . . ." And we would all burst out laughing.

The pope demonstrated a healthy and vigorous appetite, reawakened by the morning's exertions. He tried and savored everything, including a slice of apricot pie that Mom had made from scratch. I remember the pope saying he was sorry that she had to spend all her time in the kitchen, and asked for her to come out so that he could compliment her on the delicious dessert. The atmosphere was playful and jovial. Then Pertini suddenly said, "We shouldn't hide this from the world, it's just too wonderful, Your Holiness, we have to reveal that you have this passion . . . that we were here together." The pope laughed, but didn't say yes or no.

Then, at the end of the meal, while Pertini was

having a grappa and the Holy Father was drinking his coffee, Don Stanislao said, "Sure, why not, people would love to know how beautiful your friendship is!"

No sooner said than done. Pertini and I got up and went to the room where the radio transmitter was. We called the barracks of the carabinieri in Pinzolo, with which we had a dedicated connection. The commander, the agreeable Marshal Luciano Colombo, a man of unquestionable character, answered. In his usual abrupt and impetuous style, Pertini actually grabbed the microphone out of my hands and said in a loud, clear voice, "Marshal, this is your president, start writing!"

Colombo thought it was a joke, someone imitating Pertini's voice, and interrupted him: "You all quit drinking up there already, I've got enough of a hassle with this bomb-clearing business . . ."

At this point Pertini handed the microphone back to me, and I patiently explained that this was not a joke—but Colombo took an awful lot of convincing!

Afterward he confessed to me that when the president began speaking to him again, he was struck by a sort of deference "at a distance," and snapped to attention: "At your orders. Please continue, Mr. President!"

"So then, write this. Press office of the Quirinale. Communicate to the press immediately that the Holy Father and the president of the republic are here skiing on the Adamello. No one else has been allowed to come here. We send our greetings to all the mountaineers. I also send my greetings to you, dearest marshal, together with all your men."

Naturally, the news was all over the world in a matter of minutes. Back at the table, Pertini laughed and said, "Now I really have to leave, tomorrow is the seventeenth and I don't fly on the seventeenth; I'm just superstitious that way."

The pope was even more amused at this: "Okay, so next time I'll come on the seventeenth, and you'll stay at home!"

They were always bantering back and forth like this, and it was clear how well they understood and liked each other. After lunch, around three in the afternoon, Pertini and his staff prepared to leave. The pope hugged the president tight and then walked with him to the helicopter. We were now a tiny group: my family, Don Stanislao, Monsignor Taddeo, Angelo Gugel, and Cibin and a few of his men.

The pope went to his room to rest, while the news of this exceptional event was echoing around the world, piquing the curiosity of millions and millions of people. The Adamello was besieged by journalists and other curious people, kept well away from us by the security forces scattered all over the territory. Isolated from the world, we knew nothing about this yet, and we didn't care. The pope came back down at around four o'clock. His face was rested and slightly red from the sun. His energy was back. He was in a great mood, and he wanted to go skiing again right away.

It was a magnificent day at the height of summer, there was still plenty of sunshine, and the afternoon was just barely starting to turn colder. My brother Franco and I decided to take the pope to a different side of the mountain, because the snow was more compact there in the afternoon. My dad took us to the right spot on the snowcat. We got off, and before we put our skis on we showed the pope the magnificent view of the mountain peaks: Cime delle Tre Lobbie, the Conca Mandrone, the Ortles, and the summit of the Adamello, the Presanella. The light was beautiful, already turning colors, and the sky was full of picturesque clouds. As I talked I mentioned the Cresta Croce, that beautiful, lonesome rock spur so dear to us who lived there. The pope asked me why it was called Cresta Croce. I told the story:

Your Holiness, the name comes from an old cross that seems to have been placed on that steep rocky crag right around the year 1900. The story is that it was set up as an act of piety and devotion after the death of a young shepherd who fell to his death in a deep crevasse nearby. In any case, since then that Christian symbol has become a spiritual destination for mountain climbers. And it seems to have been a point of reference for soldiers during the war. Of course, that cross is very important to us, and we are very much attached to it, even if it is so flimsy and unsteady that it almost seems like a miracle that it has stood for so long. You will be able to see it again later from the window in your room, because it's only a few hundred yards from our lodge as the crow flies.

He insisted on more details about the cross.

"It is made up of two slender, plain tree trunks." I said. "They have become so discolored and polished that they look like cork, but they last. Maybe it's because the cold penetrating into the wood discolors it, but also makes it stronger, almost impermeable to the environment."

I also referred to the famous 149G cannon nick-named, "Hippopotamus," which was heroically brought all the way up there by the alpine soldiers. I explained how it took superhuman efforts to accomplish the proj-ect, how men, sleds, and horses had dragged it up to Cresta Croce at the risk of death. I showed him the Cima Venerocolo below, where they dragged it back down to in just one night.

He seemed very interested, and even profoundly moved by those stories, and from time to time, as we skied around the surrounding area for the next three hours, he would ask for details on those hardships of the alpine sol-diers. I did not go into much detail then about the history of the "Hippopotamus." But it is a wonderful story, even epic, so I will dwell on it for a bit now, faithfully follow-ing an account of that time. On the morning of February 9, the cannon left from Temù, my home town, dragged by horses. That evening it reached Malga Caldea (5,200 feet),where the road of Val d'Avio ended. The snowdrifts were high, and from there the load could continue only on sleds. It was broken down into its components: the barrel (which weighed more than three and a half tons), the mount, and the wheels. The barrel and the mount were placed on strong, custom-built wooden sleds. It was guided by a few officers commanding about sixty artillery troops and thirteen combat engineers, assisted by two hundred alpine soldiers and infantrymen. A swarm of men bustled and strained around the "Hippopotamus." A corporal went in front, carrying on his shoulders the big double rope attached to the load, and identified the exact place where the trail was to be tamped down with paddles by men. A few yards from the soldier who rhythmically tugged on the big ropes, two soldiers stood beside each sled and held guide lines to keep the loads from falling into the snow. Behind the huge sled on which the enormous barrel was placed, one and sometimes two soldiers, using a heavy iron bar, kept the load from slipping backward. It took strenuous effort, because they had to follow the steepest possible course, since the zigzag route could cause the big sled to fall over. The load frequently sank into the snow and got stuck. Winches and pulleys were used to make the load easier to pull. Naturally, the train of sleds proceeded at an exasperatingly slow pace, especially because the work could be done only at night, or when clouds or mist kept the enemy from spotting it by air.

During the daytime, when the sky was clear, the train was stopped and shovelfuls of snow were thrown on top of the sleds, while the soldiers, using big fir branches as brooms, erased the tracks that had been left. It took about twenty days to climb the 1,300 feet between the Malga Caldea and the Malga Laghetto, since this meant going up the three waterfalls of the Avio tributary, which had frozen into steep chutes.

The weather took a turn for the worse in March: for almost two weeks, the snow fell hard and the storms raged. The main load had to be halted, but all of the accessory material was transported by cable car.

The danger of avalanches was very real, and on various occasions snowdrifts buried the cannon, requiring the soldiers to go to exhausting lengths to free it from the thick blanket of snow. The weather finally improved in April, and the caravan got moving again.

The task somehow became worse over the stretch called "Calvary." The men were weary in body and spirit. Not even the periodic distribution of refreshment (wine, Marsala, grappa, sambuca) was able to reinvigorate their activity. What spurred them on instead, increasing their energy and their sense of duty and military solidarity, was seeing the wounded and dead who were brought down to the valley after the bloody battles in the middle of April. Aware of the importance of their contribution to the next battle, they clenched their jaws and began pulling with all their might, so that by April 17 the cannon was at the Garibaldi shelter (8,300 feet).

The soldiers traversed the next two thousand feet,

to the Passo Venerocolo, where the cannon was to be set up, in ten days. On April 27, 1916, the cannon was in position, just in time to support a new and large-scale attack. It would remain on the Venerocolo for more than a year, until on the night of June 6, 1917, two hundred alpine soldiers and artillerymen, going over the Passo della Tredicesima, dragged it all the way down to the pass of Cresta Croce (10,800 feet), where it can still be seen today.

As I said, while we were skiing Pope John Paul II again asked me about the cross, and whether it was a point of reference for the faith of the local population. I told him that it was, emphasizing that it was the focus of prayers for the deceased, when thoughts would go out to all those poor departed still buried under the blanket of the perennial snows. He interrupted me, and said that we should say a prayer of our own for those poor dead soldiers. We did so. Then I resumed explaining how all of us, since we were children, had had to come to terms with that sorrowful past, frequently coming across visible signs of the Great War. I told him that we often found barbed wire, scraps of clothing and shoes, mule carcasses, and unfortunately, human remains.

I added that the cross also represented something beautiful and special for me and my family, since it seemed to protect our lodge from above. The pope was deeply moved, and once again he spoke with Don Stanislao quietly and in Polish. After the last slope, he asked if we could say a prayer in the direction of Cresta Croce.

He became intent once again, and we recited a number of Hail Marys together with him. It made me curious that he did not offer any other prayers, as he did in the morning, except to the Blessed Mother. It is only now that I realize how this corresponds with a precise logic, which I could not understand at the time. We went back to the lodge at around seven, and he appeared even happier about enjoying the family atmosphere. We sat down out on the terrace, on the bench, for tea. He did so with evident enjoyment, in part because, as I had noticed, he needed to eat small, light meals. Even when we were skiing, he would bring along a couple of cookies or two slices of bread with some ham. The operation on his intestine, a result of his injury in the assassination attempt, had made this way of eating necessary for him. As the doctors said, "Little, and often."

While we were sitting there, he asked about the cross again. It was right there in front of us, boldly standing out against the pale blue sky, which had already begun to take on the softer shades of sunset. My brother Franco was also sitting there with us, and two or three close friends who had gone skiing with us. He asked them the very same questions he had asked me, wanting more details about that wooden cross, about how it had been made, about who had put it there and when. He seemed almost anxious to hear someone else repeat what I had told him, as if compiling a precise account. He then returned to that afternoon's conversation. I can still hear his voice in my ears: "But this cross is of wood, what kind of wood?"

We went inside and I showed him a photo of the cross that was hanging on the wall in one of the rooms in the lodge. He took it in his hands and looked at it for a long time. Then he spent a few minutes in silence, as if absorbed in his thoughts. Everyone who was there will remember this detail very clearly: everyone was overflowing with descriptions and explanations, while he remained silent, I would say disturbed, by that old cross made with two slender trunks, still wrapped in a bark eroded by the wind until it had become like cork. Then he went to his room to change, and came down shortly afterward. He was wearing a gray shirt and dark pants, with his hair combed slightly backward. He went to the kitchen, where Mom was preparing dinner.

He chatted with her there, sitting on a chair in the corner like an old man waiting for the women to get everything ready. The image seems unreal to me today: a pope, a future saint, a man who held the fate of the Catholic Church in his hands, sitting next to the stove, wiling away the time in the kitchen at my house. If I didn't have the photos with our pots hanging on the wall, sometimes I might think it had been a dream. I remember that he and Don Stanislao laughed about the comments, the curiosity, the excitement that Pertini's press release must have created in the world of journalism.

"Who knows what they'll say, what comments they will make, that the president and I were here on vacation," John Paul mused.

We turned on the television, which was in the kitchen, in time for the eight o'clock news. The news began with this headline: "The pope and Pertini together to ski on the Adamello." Then the pope, addressing my mother, began asking for more details about our family: if the grandparents were still alive, how many years she had been married to my father, if my sister's marriage was going well, if any of the rest of us were engaged, how work was going. . . . It was clear that he was not just making small talk, but that he was sincerely interested in the details of the family harmony. After awhile, we left them there chatting in a corner by themselves. It was apparent that he wanted a moment alone with her. And my mother still talks about how he suddenly went silent, as if too sad to speak. She went to Don Stanislao and told him, "Maybe the Holy Father doesn't feel well, his expression changed, it was like he became sad all of a sudden."

He replied, "No, don't worry, Mrs. Carla. He must be thinking about his family, about his mom. He has told me that you remind him of the few happy years when his mother was alive."

So Mom went back into the kitchen and said, "Your Holiness, it's almost nine, time to come to the table."

And the pope: "Yes, but I'm not sitting down to eat

unless you come sit near me, not like today at lunch when you stayed in the kitchen."

And she did. Halfway through dinner, he made a gesture to Don Stanislao, who went to get a package and brought it back to him. He opened it himself: it was a beautiful image of the Black Madonna of Częstochowa. He placed it on the table, solemnly blessed it, and gave it to mom.

He said to her in an intensely emotional voice, "This Madonna will be with you always, she will protect your whole family and help you in every circumstance in which you need her."

Mom was deeply moved and thanked him, holding back her tears. He broke the tension by starting to explain how devoted he himself was to the Black Madonna, which was kept in Jasna Góra in Poland.

He explained that the Black Madonna was a Byzantine icon of medieval tradition. Legend has it that it was painted by Saint Luke, who, being a contemporary of the Virgin Mary, was able to depict her true face. The pope recounted that the shrine at which it was kept, in addition to being a place steeped in history, was also a place of culture, with a library that held more than forty thousand rare manuscripts. He said that in all moments of great difficulty, the Polish people came together around the Black Madonna, and that every summer tens of thousands of faithful went on foot to that place of devotion. He told us that he himself had made that pilgrimage, leaving from Krakow in 1936. He made reference to the possibility of obtaining a grace by praying directly to the Black Madonna:

O Mother of the Church,
with the choirs of angels and our holy patrons,
we humbly prostrate ourselves before your throne.
For centuries you have shone with miracles
and graces here in Jasna Góra,
the seat of your infinite mercy.
Look upon the hearts of us who present to you
our homage of veneration and love.
Revive within us the desire for holiness;
mold us into true apostles of faith;
strengthen our love for the Church and obtain
for us this grace that we so greatly desire:
O mother of the scarred face, into your hands
I place myself and all my loved ones.
In you I confide, sure of your intercession
with your son, to the glory of the Most
Holy Trinity.
Beneath your protection we take refuge,
O Holy Mother of God:
look upon us who are in need.
Our Lady of the Luminous Mountain, pray for us.
Amen.

As I write down these memories and reflections twenty-six years later, the icon of the Black Madonna represents a comfort for my family, which is going through a particularly sorrowful situation. It has always hung in the bedroom of my mother and father, Carla and Martino. Once again I cannot help but thank God for the great spiritual resources that that man, His messenger, brought to my family, above all at moments like this.

Unlike lunch, the dinner was frugal. The pope, already at his ease as if part of the family, had said without standing on ceremony what he would like to eat. He had soup and ate a little piece of alpine cheese that he had already tried at lunch. When the fruit came he had just a slice of apple, and to finish he asked for a teaspoon—and he really meant just a teaspoon—of Fernet (an herb liquor often used as a digestif), which he sipped slowly, as if it were medicine. At the end of the dinner, the pope suddenly stood up and said, "Excuse me, but I have to finish my prayers. I'm going to my room."

We all stayed outside chatting, careful to keep the noise down so as not to disturb him. Looking up to his window, I realized that he had not closed the shutters. It was still light outside, because up where we were the night comes later, and a pale blue dusky glow remains for a long time, giving in to the darkness very late. From the window of his room, the cross of Cresta Croce, that slender cross, was perfectly visible, as if crowning the view like a cornice. Today I am absolutely certain that, in retiring with such sudden haste, as if overcome, he must have wanted to be alone in the presence of that cross, an emblem that was to become ever more present in his life.

At about 6:30 the following morning, we all gathered around him in the dining room for Mass. He celebrated it before breakfast. It was a brief Mass, but particularly intense because of the pope was the celebrant. We all took Communion, receiving the Eucharist from his hands with visible emotion. The evening before, I had asked Don Stanislao to hear my confession.

In the homily, the pope talked about the casualties of the Adamello, and asked us to pray frequently for those poor dead men who were buried and forgotten there. He ate breakfast with a hearty appetite. Milk, coffee, bread, and cheese, and then a little treat that he had requested: the evening before, he had showered Mom with compliments and told her how much he would like to have another piece of that delicious pie. She was very pleased, and even got up at four o'clock in the morning to bake it, so that it would be nice and fresh. The pope enjoyed it immensely. He got up from the table to get another slice, and Don Stanislao pretended to chide him: "But Your Holiness, what are you doing, eat at the table, put the pie on your plate."

The pope replied, laughing, "Why, in the hands like this is no good? My hands make a great plate, my mom made them for me."

Then he went to change. He put his skiing clothes back on and set aside his sacred vestments. When he came back down, he told my mom he was leaving them there, whispering to her, "These will be a keepsake for you. They will be used by the priests who come up here to say Mass."

Angelo, his personal assistant, then asked Mom to tidy up his room personally, and not let in anyone else. There had been a great deal of apprehension the night before on the part of many. First among them was our dear Marshal Colombo, who had found himself, after Pertini's press release, facing an extremely complicated situation with limited resources and very few men. As the hours went by, many people had begun a sort of "siege" of the Adamello, trying to meet the pope. The surrounding mountains were crawling with journalists, photographers, local residents, members of the faithful, or mere curiosity seekers who had come with the hope of going up to the lodge. The greatest source of concern, apart from the pope's safety, was the very real danger that someone, out of a lack of caution or a lack of expertise, might get into trouble trying to climb the glacier without knowing the territory. The ascent of a glacier at an elevation of more than ten thousand feet is not for the inexperienced: there are the crevasses, slippery ice, and weather that can change in an instant.

At dawn, while the Holy Father was still resting in his room, security officers advised us that overnight two men had gotten past the roadblock and the security perimeter, and had come close to the lodge. I went to find out who they were. Fortunately I knew them. They were a journalist of the newspaper, *Adige*, and a local guide, a man who lived in Giustino, a town not far away from us. We then informed the pope of the episode, and he asked us to let them come up: they had walked all night in the cold, and since the temperature drops below zero at night, it was our duty to get them fed and warm. The Holy Father seemed rather amused, greeting them pleasantly and asking them to tell him in detail how they had managed to get around the security measures. They told him with visible emotion: they had started from the Mandrone glacier, climbing through the area between trail 236 and the "Ferramenta."

Smiling, the pope interrupted: "Okay, we're going skiing now. But I see that you are very tired, you've walked all night, you should go rest."

He asked that a room be provided for them, and had Mom go with them: "Mrs. Carla, make sure that they rest well and for a long time, because they're very tired and they shouldn't go out!"

He had sorted them out, and could be confident that they would not follow us on the slopes. But he embraced with great and paternal affection another who had snuck up to the lodge: the young alpine conscript Gabriele Pedretti, from Carisolo. He was the son of our dear friend Faustino, the owner of a local rock quarry. Faustino is a man of great faith who, a few years later, would accomplish the titanic feat of building something that the Holy Father desired. The pope liked Gabriele immediately, in part because as a young man he himself had worked at a rock quarry in Poland. He knew very well how hard that work was! And so the "little alpine," who had just turned twenty, took a place of affection in the pope's memory.

Without saying anything to his superiors, Gabriele had sneaked away from the barracks by night and after walking for hours had presented himself, at dawn on that morning of July 17, 1984, near one of the barricades set up to protect the Holy Father.

He said that he was a friend of the family, and that he had an immense desire to pay his respects to the pope. But try as he might to convince them, he was about to be sent back. Another friend of the family, the carabiniere Rino Pedergnana, intervened on his behalf and asked Marshal Colombo that he be given special permission to go up. Again the answer was no, and he said angrily, "He is an alpine . . . and when they die, they don't even have time to make the sign of the cross!"

Two hours later, the "little alpine" was with the pope, who clasped him in an affectionate embrace for a keepsake photo. Shortly afterward, however, I saw how a pope and a future saint can get angry, even very angry. The pope's staff told him that the security situation was spinning out of control. On top of that, the forecasts said that the weather was about to turn bad.

His expression became very stern, and he spoke urgently with Don Stanislao in Polish. In a matter of minutes a regrettable but necessary decision had been made. For obvious reasons, he would leave early, departing that evening instead of the following day. Although he was very displeased, his good mood returned when he walked out the door and saw that in spite of everything it was another beautiful day, with sparkling sunshine gleaming on the snow. He wanted to go back to ski on the slopes of Cresta Croce, where we had been the day before. We got back onto the snowcat, crossing an area from which we could see the peak of Carè Alto, at an elevation of 11,358 feet. The pope was clearly shaken when he heard the name, and told us a secret: "It is here, it is right here that my father fought. The Poles, if such a thing is possible, were treated even worse than the others, they were given the worst jobs."

We saw that he was deeply moved, and we left him alone for a few minutes, to look out the window and reminisce about his father. It was only some time later that I learned that there was a prison and a little wooden church a few dozen yards from the shelter of Caré Alto, built by a group of Russian-Polish prisoners. An old military trail goes up the east side of the Caré Alto, and leads, after an hour's walk, to the "cannon mouth," at an elevation of 9,379 feet.

Aside from the pope's few words, I never heard of or read in any publication even a mention of his father's experience in the war. Perhaps he himself never spoke of it in detail, deciding to reveal such an intimate aspect of his family history only to me, in those truly special moments and days.

With our skis now back on our feet, I again saw in his eyes the pure joy of a man reinvigorated by the open air, by elements of nature that were completely agreeable to him. Again, I saw his happiness caused by the freedom in the speed of the descent, the little hazards, the boldness of the sportsman enjoying his own mastery, becoming one with his surroundings. At noon we recited the Angelus, and immediately afterward we talked about the war again. He asked me about the ruins of the citadel that the slowly retreating glaciers spit back out in the summer. He asked how those barracks, towers, and basements were laid out. I tried to be more exact and to tell him in detail everything I knew. I explained that the barracks stood all around our lodge, spaced out over twenty miles or so. I reiterated that the lodge itself stood on what had been a barracks, and perhaps even a prison. Over the three long years of that terrible conflict, because of the obvious need to build shelter to protect the poor soldiers from their number one enemy, the cold, it had been necessary to build a vast complex of wooden cabins. I added that there were also some more sophisticated constructions. In short, it was a sort of fortified citadel, with underground walkways and areas carved into the rock.

I explained that a tunnel three miles long, equipped with eighty ventilation ducts, connected the Passo Garibaldi with the Passo della Lobbia, crossing twenty-five crevasses. I told him about the avalanches, another grave danger that the soldiers had to face, a phenomenon that in the winter of 1916–1917 claimed even more victims than the combat did.

For this reason, one cannot fully understand the drama of the Great War without also taking into account the tens of thousands who died in avalanches, who were frozen, who endured the unspeakable sufferings of men forced simply to survive before they could fight. I am reminded of the time when they explained to us at school how the first alpine troops, deployed at the extremely high elevations of our mountains, were still wearing the linen uniforms of the war in Libya—at ten thousand feet!

I told the pope the story, just as I had heard it from our elders, of the great valor of the two corps: the alpine soldiers on one side, and the Tiroler Kaiserjaeger on the other. Many of the peaks in the battle had, and still have, frightening precipices. Many soldiers, having run out of ammunition, were plunged into the void during desperate hand-to-hand combat. I made mention of the shrines that had been set up in all the local cemeteries for the collection of the remains of soldiers. I told the pope how, for many of them, the glaciers would forever be their graves. In the same way, our grandfathers had told us that many of the alpines chosen to fight at high altitudes came from our area, recruited from among the farmers, shepherds, and mountain people who knew the terrain and had in their hearts the spirit of defending the territory. Even without considering the country's borders, they wanted to protect their own towns, their own communities, and above all their modest farmland carved out of the high plains and the alpine pastures.

I told him that the women also participated in the war: the wives, mothers, sweethearts, and relatives of the soldiers provided them with food and personal items. They put their own lives in danger in order to bring supplies to the troops scattered around the peaks. All of this had a tremendous impact on John Paul. I saw great suffering in his eyes, and I would have liked to stop telling him those sad stories—after all, we were there to ski. It was a beautiful day, and the last of his vacation. But he continued to ask me questions, to dig for details, to ask for more.

As I told the head of the Catholic Church the stories of this immense historical tragedy of humanity, I was reminded of something he had once said: "The only war worthy of man is the war against war!"

I had the strange sensation, immediate and profound, that all of this seemed to concern him very intimately. I thought of his father's involvement, of how much he must have missed him. And this was certainly true, or at least plausible. But now I know that there was more, much more!

There was something deep in his heart, the kernel of a truth that was making inroads into his mind. Something that would come to form the foundation of a special bond that he would later form with me.

Something he had been thinking of for some time, and that he would find confirmed in my words, without me even realizing it. Many times over the years to come I would see that John Paul II's affection for me and my family was something more than the usual testimony of a strong and supportive friendship. That "something more" was being created right then, at the time of our first encounter on the Adamello. Long afterward, while conversing about one of the expeditions that have led me to climb some of the highest mountains in the world, he asked me the point-blank question: "Lino, who or what drives you to get to the top of those mountains, why do you do it?"

I answered him: "Because I like to understand and discover what is beyond, and when I arrive up there at the top, it seems to me that I can understand. I have a different perspective on things."

He said, "It's the same for me. We're both looking for the same thing, that's why we understand each other." But then he added, and I will never forget it, "But remember that when you get to the top, you can only go down. Man can go only so high!" Now I understand that it's true.

On the morning of July 17, the bags were prepared and everything was ready for the pope's departure in the afternoon. At the very moment that the helicopters arrived and all of the preparations had been made by the carabinieri of Pinzolo, something unexpected happened.

In the early afternoon, the pope changed his mind. He had put his skiing clothes back on, and, coming down from his room, he asked Dad, "So then, Martino, could you maybe take me for one more quick run?" Out in the front yard, he took me aside: "Lino, would you take me up to Cresta Croce again?"

We left behind the authorities, the helicopters, the agents, and his staff. A change was made to the schedule of the airplane in Verona that would take him back to Rome. Today the pope's desire for one more run, in the light of everything that would take place in the years to come, remains wonderful to me. That afternoon he just skied. He didn't ask any more questions, and he didn't reveal any particular emotion. He simply seemed happy to be there, and perhaps a bit displeased that he had to leave. He observed everything with extreme attention, almost as if he wanted to fix forever in his mind and in his heart every detail of the magnificent landscape stretching all the way to the horizon.

During his last run, he wanted to stop for just five minutes to pray in front of the tower that we call "the observatory," right above the citadel, and then we were on our way. When we returned we found everyone waiting for us. In addition to various authorities who had come to pay their respects, the family that had been sent away at his arrival because of our excuse that old wartime munitions were being detonated there. After he had found out about them, the pope expressly asked for them to come so that he could wish them a pleasant continuation of their vacation.

He went back to his room to change, and then we all accompanied him to the helicopter, with a feeling of regret that we couldn't have him with us for at least one more day. I remember the moment when I again bent down to kiss his hand and he stopped me, said an affectionate goodbye, and then said to me in his unmistakable voice, "Lino, I'll be expecting you soon at the Vatican. You and your whole family, your wonderful family." The blades of the big helicopter whirred into motion, drowning out the loud goodbyes and the shouts of joy. The good marshal, Luciano Colombo, who had done so much to guarantee the pope's safety, wrote in a note:

> John Paul II left at 7:30 pm on 7/17/1984.

The bell, a symbol of the "fallen of the Adamello," began to ring, and those vibrations, fraught with emotion followed us to where the glacier ends. We all felt a sense of melancholy, as if a dear friend had suddenly left us. We stopped into the little church of the Mandrone without knowing why. Those who prayed, prayed, and those who did not know any prayers murmured a word of thanksgiving. It was faith, which, from deep within, was knocking at the doors of our hearts. When he disappeared from our view, we all felt worn out and desired to be alone. Everyone said a quick goodbye and went to their homes. All of a sudden it seemed that a great void had been created around us.

We did not speak much with each other, everyone wanted a little solitude, and we went our own ways without talking about it. All of a sudden I felt extremely tired, more so than if I had climbed one of my mountains. That night in bed I did a sort of inventory: of his smiles, of his gestures, of his expressions, and of his questions. It was normal to be emotional after having met a pope, and this sensation united everyone who had been present.

But I sensed that it was not only that shared experience. For me, there was something more, like an implicit reference, mysterious and yet extremely clear for my life. I perceived a sense of responsibility, and at the same time, a sense of amazement over a bond so strong that it had been created over a few hours. I thought that I would never see him again, except perhaps at a distance. If I was lucky, maybe I would be able to attend a celebration with him at the Vatican. That would be logical. But I felt that another intimate meeting was impossible. There had been such fellowship with my family, such a sincere exchange of affection. And with me, an encounter of the eyes, his piercing like hooks into mine, good and kind but capable of shaking you to the core. And then the two of us talking and all that snow around us, which, little by little, as I told him about those who had died, seemed to become stained red with their blood.

I was home, in my own territory, and I had heard

those stories and told them to others thousands of times, and yet I felt that I was inside them as never before, as if the pope and I had spoken of things that had happened not a century before, but just days ago.

It was as if all of that suffering and pain had been transferred onto me, by means of a mysterious process of spiritual communication. And the cross kept coming back into my mind. I was unable to erase it from my sight. It stood out sharply against that little piece of sky that could be seen from the window that for one night had been his. With its shutters unlatched, thrown wide open to the universe, to that world full of all the suffering of the past, and to thoughts known to him alone.

I got up and went to that room, threw open the window, and looked for the pinnacle of rock and the cross planted there. But it had already been swallowed up in the darkness of the night. I couldn't see a thing. The thought came to me, I don't know why, that he had taken it with him, and I seemed to see it in my mind's eye: so crude and plain, so eaten away as to resemble cork, there among the opulent splendors of the Vatican: the gold, the statues, the saints, the marble columns, all the beauty of the Renaissance, and that poor, miserable cross, an eyesore to the angels.

That night, however, there was just the darkness, and my peaceful solitude. But when I looked up at the sky, I saw a breathtaking display of stars, as if they had all arranged to arrive that one night. I raised my hand as if to touch them, they appeared so close. It seemed like a good sign.

In the following days I went to a photographer, a close friend, to have him develop the photos that we had taken. They were intense and beautiful, truly encapsulating all of the emotions we had felt and capturing the memories of remarkable, unforgettable days. After the pope left, we were assailed by the media from all over the world. Newspapers offered to buy the photos, and the story of those moments. They offered dizzying figures, but we refused to release any statement at all, let alone an image. But I didn't know what to do—I had taken those photos so that the pope could have them as a keepsake, too, but instead they had remained in my possession. Don Stanislao had given me his direct telephone number at the Vatican, so I decided to call him.

His joy at hearing from me again was clear and sincere, it seemed that I was reconnecting with an old friend, and I was immensely happy about it. When I explained my problem, that I was being hounded by the newspapers, he said immediately, "Don't worry about it, come to Rome and I'll take care of it, I'll be waiting for you."

I got on a plane and went to Rome to meet with him. We had coffee in his office and had a pleasant conversation about our days on the Adamello. Once again he told me that the pope had been very happy. Then we selected a few photos together, just a dozen or so. These were given to the press: the pope skiing alone, one of him with me and Pertini, one of just Pertini and him. It goes without saying that they met with unprecedented publicity, since they brought curiosity, enjoyment, and tenderness to readers all over the world. It was extraordinary to see a pope and a president looking as happy as a couple of kids playing hooky to go have fun in the mountains! Don Stanislao gave the rest of the photos back to me, saying, "We have greatly appreciated your confidentiality, these photos are yours to use as you wish, we trust you."

I thanked him warmly for his trust, and promised him, "I will keep these photos for no one but us, for our family album; as long as the Holy Father is alive they will remain private keepsakes, as will the story of those days, which for now must remain ours alone!" Years have gone by, and the promise was kept.

Even after the death of John Paul II, I didn't feel like sharing those stories and images. It really is true that there is a season for everything. But as soon as I found out about his beatification, I felt that the time had come: he would be happy about this now. And for the first time I opened the floodgates of my memories, which came rushing down like an avalanche.

V

# SIGNS OF HOLINESS

IN SEPTEMBER, a couple of months after the encounter on the Adamello, my brother Franco and I went to Rome to see the pope at the Vatican. The appointment had been organized in an informal and hasty manner thanks to the intercession of trusty Don Stanislao.

It was wonderful to see the Holy Father again. We were very emotional, and he, in an excellent mood, cracked one joke after another, entertaining us with his subtle irony. We spent half an hour with him, and later found out that this had meant keeping an African head of state waiting. We came away lighthearted, thinking how great it was to have a pope as a friend.

It was even more thrilling to meet with him shortly before Christmas of that same year. Around the middle of December, we received a telephone call informing us that the Holy Father would like us to visit his private quarters for an Advent Mass and to exchange Christmas greetings. We were specifically told that he wanted to see the whole family.

The preparations began: proper attire, travel arrangements, accommodations. Apart from me, there were my parents, Carla and Martino, my brother Franco and his wife, our sister Renata and her husband, and our younger sister, Miriam. The appointment was set for seven in the morning on December 22. Our alarm clock went off two hours early, even though we were staying very close to the Vatican, in a hotel on the Via della Conciliatzione. We were all tremendously excited. It was one thing to attend the Mass said there at our house, like a simple family prayer or an Easter blessing. It was another thing to be admitted to the most important liturgy in the world, there in the heart of Christendom. What we would have to say and do, how we would have to do it, when we would speak, how we would approach him and the Eucharist—it all seemed so complicated. And yet everything would turn out to be beautiful, solemn, and simple.

We entered through the Bronze Gate, to the right of the colonnade, climbed the grand stone staircase, and passed the checkpoint of the Swiss Guards, dressed in their distinctive colorful uniforms. We walked across the courtyard of Saint Damasus, a highly evocative spot that has seen kings, queens, and heads of state from all over the world pass through it. We went up to the third floor of the apostolic palace, and walked down the hallway on the left, the one of the Third Loggia. From there we entered the pope's private quarters. We went through a door into a wide vestibule leading to a sitting room next to the private library. We were made to wait in the little office reserved for Don Stanislao. He welcomed us himself, and after we greeted each other joyfully he brought us into the pope's private study, at the window of which he appeared every Sunday to recite the Angelus, and where he gave the *Urbi et Orbi* blessings.

We then entered the private chapel next to the pope's bedroom. He was already in place, in his white cassock and green vestments. We took our places in silence. In addition to us, there were about twenty priests of various nationalities, who were about to leave for mission territories. If one were to ask me what morning Mass with the pope is like, and what procedures are followed, or how long it lasts, I could only reply that it is a truly religious ceremony marked by the greatest simplicity, yet very intense.

There was no trace of official imposition, no embarrassment, and we suddenly realized that it was entirely natural for us to be there all together, intent on watching him, attentive to his movements and their spiritual message. The only peculiarity of that Mass was that there was no homily. Before the consecration of the Eucharist, the pope recollected himself in deep meditation. It was a moment of intense absorption, although less pronounced than what I had seen when he was sitting on the rock at the top of the Passo di Lares.

* * * * *

Many times, especially as his beatification was approaching, I asked myself what were the signs of his holiness. I have tried to shed light on them, poring over my memories to understand better. I have tried to do this with lucidity, with a spirit of observation and rationality, without getting carried away by emotion. And so I can assert with absolute certainty that one of the signs that I encountered was precisely what he was able to transmit to those who had the immense privilege of attending one of those intense, anguished, weighty prayer sessions. It was as if he took hold of the hearts of those present, as if he changed the structure of time and place.

Here's an example: it could have been a few minutes or even hours, but afterward one had the sense that everything had happened fast, like lightning. What lasted the whole day and even much longer was, instead, a sensation of peace, of floating over all the things of life. It was as if one had succeeded in distancing oneself from problems, anxieties, and worries, although without having forgotten them.

The main effect of his holiness was precisely that of transmitting a stream of unexpected courage to face one's own life, whatever it was like. For a little while after having been with him, one became intrepid, impermeable to the evil of sufferings, unharmed by fear.

"Be not afraid! Open, rather, throw the doors wide

open for Christ." You will remember that he had already said this on that Sunday of October 22, 1978, the day of his installation.

After the Mass, we were led out of the private chapel and accompanied to a room across from the dining room. The pope changed, said goodbye to the other guests, and came back to us, greeting each of us very warmly, one by one. He then told us that he would like us to have breakfast together.

We went into the adjacent dining room, where the table was already set. Don Stanislao, naturally, was also present. We were served milk, coffee, and tea, and some exquisite homemade coffee cakes prepared by the Polish sisters of the Congregation of the Sacred Heart, who together with their superior, Tobiana Sobodka, always took care of John Paul II with love and discretion. They were the ones who served us at table, attentive but not intrusive, and gentle, like real guardian angels. As always, the pope showed an interest in each one of us, calling us by name and asking for news and details about everyone. He wanted to know how things were going, how work and life were up there on the mountain. He asked us how we were going to spend the Christmas holidays, and dwelt with evident pleasure upon his memories of the Adamello, or rather "our Adamello," as he would call it from then on.

We left the Vatican with the sensation of having been in a dream: our whole family at breakfast with

Pope John Paul II, perhaps the most beloved man in the world. Being able to converse with him as if he were a member of the family truly seemed to us the fruit of an extraordinary privilege. My mom, my sister-in-law, and my dad let loose with long and enthusiastic commentaries on the solemnity of the places we had just visited, on the unique beauty of the buildings and their interiors.

All true, but afterward I would hear in person from "my" pope how that place, so rich in history and magnificence, sometimes represented a real prison for him. At the Vatican, the successor of Peter exercised his mission as Supreme Pontiff with complete abnegation, but the man rediscovered during those moments of rest and contemplation in the mountains his most authentic spiritual closeness to God. It was therefore an immense privilege to have been a witness and companion of his trips to the mountain, in search of the exhilaration of freedom, but also of the essential, of his most authentic relationship with God.

Nearly four years later, at the beginning of the spring of 1988, I went to see him again because I was about to leave on an important expedition in Asia. I was going to climb Cho Oyu, a mountain with an elevation of 26,906 feet, situated on the border between Tibet and Nepal, a few miles from Everest. I arrived at the Vatican in the morning, and again I was admitted into his quarters to attend Mass in his private chapel. Then we had a long conversation about my upcoming adventure. He was very curious about my trip, and asked me how I would approach the climb and how I had prepared. He also wanted to know why I had chosen Cho Oyu.

I spoke to him about it at length, explaining to him that it was the sixth-highest mountain in the world, but above all that it presented breathtaking colors and views during the climb. In fact, "Cho Oyu" means "Turquoise Goddess" in Tibetan. I explained that once one reached the terminal plateau at an elevation of about 18,536 feet, one could observe up close the marvelous northern face of Everest. He also asked me about the dangers the climb presented. I told him that the greatest danger might be constituted by the ease with which one could get lost in case of fog or low visibility, from fifteen thousand feet up, in the section of the terminal plateau. Once one was past the initial rocky section, in fact, a rather flat and even stretch of terrain followed, with few visual reference points, which could cause confusion and obscure one's sense of direction. I explained to him that like all the Himalayan mountains, this giant was not to be underestimated, and that confronting it required adequate preparation, acclimatization, and technical preparation. He listened to me with great interest, I would say almost with a touch of jealousy. It was clear that under other circumstances he would have liked to have been in my place. I would later learn how many of his memories were connected to the Tatra mountains in Poland. He told me about his camping trips, about the fact that they were coed, something very unusual for those times, and how those rocky surroundings had inspired his play *The Jeweler's Shop*.

He would also tell me, with a certain touch of pride, about his and his friends' agility canoeing over rapids, which are numerous and very swift. But I would learn about these memories of his in the years to come, when our relationship had been founded on a certain confidence. That day, however, after a long moment of reflection and silence, he said to me, "I will give you a cross to plant on that mountain. From now on, you will be our 'apostle of the mountains.' You must take a cross to the highest and most beautiful mountains of the world. Carrying the cross of Jesus on the mountains must be your mission."

I was deeply struck by those words—speechless. I didn't know what to say. But he, as usual, wasted no time and moved into action, He immediately sent for a green case from which he took a cross, about eight inches long. He blessed it and gave it to me. He said goodbye, telling me to be careful and to let him know as soon as I got back to Italy.

I got in touch with him three months later. I had endured exhaustion, the cold, storms, and temperatures of sixty degrees below zero. I had spent days and nights stuck at altitudes of over twenty thousand feet, with the wind preventing me from even sticking my head out of the tent. I had thought, as always happens, about giving up, but I was determined—and this is a switch that often "clicks" on in the heads of climbers—to reach the goal, to make it to the end no matter what. At 27,000 feet I felt a boundless sense of intoxication. I greeted the northeast face of Shisha Pangma, and in front of me was Everest.

On the summit of Cho Oyu, I planted the cross on a tripod that the Chinese had placed on the highest point. I placed it there and it seemed to me that the pope, with his immaterial yet very real presence within me, was beside me and was looking at me. I set up the camera to take a photo in that beautiful and unrepeatable moment. After I returned I went to Rome and gave the picture to the pope. He was rather touched, and said, "You see, you did it. Now you really have become the 'apostle of the mountains'!"

* * * * *

Sometimes during the winter the pope went skiing, even just for a day, on the mountains of Abruzzo, in Pescasseroli or Ovindoli, or on the nearby Mount Terminillo.

I would accompany him sometimes, and we would put our skis on right away and ski for hours, at any pace, with tremendous pleasure. Most of the time the few people we saw didn't even recognize the pope, dressed as he was in athletic gear and with his eyes concealed by sunglasses. Now and again something quite funny would happen. I remember one morning when we passed a boy of about eight years old a couple times on the ski lift. He kept looking at the pope, who smiled gently at him. At a certain point, after two or three runs, the boy came up to us and asked him point-blank, "Are you the pope?"

"Yes, do you want to ski with me?"

They rode up together several times, one behind the other on the little seats, while I enjoyed the incredible scene from a distance. I remember that at a certain point the boy went over to his mother, who was sunning herself in a chair down in the valley near the bottom of the ski lift, and shouted, "Mom, did you know I'm skiing with the pope?"

The lady just shook her head. John Paul was highly amused, and late in the morning he wanted to go say hello to her. I will never forget that woman's flabbergasted expression—even today, she must wonder if it was all a dream!

What were not dreams at all, but intense moments of prayer and meditation, were the moments I saw over and over again, always in the mountains and always after he had made a sudden decision. He may have been joyful, bubbly, invigorated by our skiing, but all of a sudden his expression would change and turn somber, as if something was deeply troubling him. As usual, the Holy Father would speak in Polish with Don Stanislao, who would tell me, "Lino, let's look for a good spot, John Paul wants to be alone for awhile."

He usually preferred spots with views stretching out to the horizon, where he could put himself in the presence of the infinite. And that anguished immobility—that capacity of ascetical concentration that I have never seen any other human being maintain for so long—always came back. I believe that in those moments, which I witnessed in silence and with profound respect, he had genuine prophetic visions. At times, in fact, the pope came out of these meditations with a very troubled expression, in great distress, as if seized by preoccupation. In those cases Don Stanislao immediately approached him, and spoke with him quietly and in Polish.

I remember one time in particular when I witnessed a dramatic scene of this nature. I saw him come out of that sort of ecstasy in great agitation, shaken to the core. He and Don Stanislao spoke privately for a long time, and then we hurried back to where we were staying. It was summer, they were on vacation, and I had joined them there. By that time I understood immediately that something bad was about to happen.

A few hours later, the Iraqi army invaded Kuwait with one hundred thousand men and three hundred tanks, overcoming all resistance by the Emirate within a few hours. The emir of Kuwait, Jaber III Al-Ahmad Al-Jaber Al-Sabah, went into exile in Saudi Arabia with his family, while his brother Fahd was killed along with two hundred others. The Gulf War had begun.

At the time, I didn't ask myself too many questions.

Instead, I observed and accepted everything that was happening before my eyes with naturalness and in a spirit of faith. Now that various miracles have been recognized and attributed to him, I no longer have any doubts: in those moments, the man to whom I was bound by the greatest affection was no longer a mere man, but was "exercising" to be a saint. Foreknowledge is one of the gifts of the saints.

Much more would happen to me in the years to come. The Holy Father saved my life twice, but I will talk about this later. After that first vacation on the Adamello, John Paul II developed the habit of spending a few days in the mountains each year, often choosing Lorenzago di Cadore, a cheerful town in northeast Italy near the Passo della Mauria, whose history is also connected to the first world war. That territory, in fact, which constitutes a corridor of access from Veneto to Friuli, was the bloody theater of the armed defense of the people of Cadore against the Austrians. Every summer, when he was there, I went and joined the group that he called his "family": Don Stanislao, Monsignor Taddeo, Luciano Cibin, Angelo Gugel, and often Arturo Mari, his personal photographer, who with delicacy and discretion captured on film those moments of such intensity and happiness.

The pope stayed in the Castello di Mirabello, situated in the woods above the town, a gorgeous location. From there we went on fantastic excursions to the Passo della Mauria, where the Tagliamento River begins, and to the south, where stands one of the highest peaks of the Cadore region, Monte Cridola. The exquisite little sixteenth-century church of Our Lady of Refuge there was particularly dear to the Holy Father. It had been erected in supplication against the effects of the war with Maximilian of Austria, and against a terrible pestilence in the early sixteenth century.

On those occasions, every time I came, I brought the pope a special gift: a pair of hiking boots, always different. They were always on the cutting edge of technical design and used different types of animal skin or other specific materials for walking and climbing. He wore a size 11-1/2, and I was always very careful to choose the most comfortable and innovative model on the market. I remember the way his eyes looked when he was unwrapping his "surprise." He was as happy as a child, and I also remember how enthusiastically he decided to try them on right away.

One time, in the winter, I gave him instead a pair of skis that truly made him proud. There was a company that had patented a high tech model. They were monocoque, completely different from traditional skis. The novelty consisted in the way they used the skier's own weight to become more aerodynamic, increasing both speed and safety. We had had a "papal" pair made. They were completely white, and I remember that he wanted to try them out as soon as possible.

Another of his favorite destinations was Entrèves in Val d'Aosta, north of Turin, where he was invited by the local bishop and provided with good accommodations in a little house in a sunny, cheerful spot. From there, from an altitude of about four thousand feet, we went to Monte Bianco, to the cheery Val Veny and Val Ferret. At lunchtime we would always stop at a little place for a light snack, and there, reinvigorated by the food and by a nice glass of wine, we often sang mountain songs. The pope liked one folk song in particular, one that could be considered a sort of anthem of the mountain. I can still hear his wonderful voice singing, "That little bunch of flowers, that comes from the mountain."

Those mountain choruses reminded him of the vacations he took as a youngster, with his friends. That same warm and informal atmosphere, the affection among persons who had come to feel close to one another, who found the desire in the beauty of nature to create a unity of mind and a strong sense of belonging.

It was so heartening, wonderful, and instructive to see how he—a pope and a future saint—enjoyed those small, simple delights of life, as any ordinary man would do. In those years, as I have already said, my life had been marked by a wholesome joy in living, typical of a young man with energy, plans, and vitality. An exuberance that led me to be very romantic as well—to put it briefly, I often had different women beside me in those years. Beautiful young women, each of them in my life for a little while, until the arrival of the next conquest. I made no secret of this—after all, I was a free man, and like many others it always seemed to me that the next one would be even better! I talked about this aspect of my life, in all sincerity, with the pope, who was my confessor, my confidant, and my spiritual father. I recall that often when I went to see him in Rome, I would bring my latest girlfriend with me. He was friendly and paternal, and would welcome us, granting his blessing to the young woman as well. But always, and I mean always, he would take me aside and ask me the same question:

"That's not the same woman as last time, right?"

And I would reply, "Holy Father, I believe that this time she's the one, I'm in love, you'll see. . . ."

With a benevolent smile, he would say, "Lino, Lino—when are you going to get your head straight?"

In his affectionate but firm exhortation to get my head straight—meaning to settle down and start a family—there was all of the concern of the "pastor of souls," but also the indulgence of the man he had been himself, a man who had known the world, the joy of friendship, and perhaps of romantic love. His choices and his destiny had led him to make big, unusual decisions of enormous value and importance. But in my opinion, his past as a completely normal young man, as an actor and as a worker in a rock quarry, made him an even more effective "fisherman of souls."

* * * * *

The initiative to build a granite altar on the Passo della Lobbia Alta to commemorate the extraordinary visit of John Paul II to the Adamello was born from an idea of my father Martino and of Faustino Pedretti, the father of the "little alpine."

I talked with John Paul about it at the first opportunity, during a visit to the Vatican, and he was truly enthusiastic about the idea. As I guessed, the pope immediately came up with the idea to go back to the mountain once the altar was finished, to see again the places that had thrilled him so much. On the Passo della Lobbia Alta, at an elevation of ten thousand feet, there was and still is a simple barbed wire fence that marked the boundary between Italy and Austrian territory, right under the spot where the "old cross of rough-hewn trunks" stood. We decided that the altar dedicated to Pope John Paul II would be built there. We thought it was a place where the faithful, tourists, and pilgrims could gather each year to commemorate the Supreme Pontiff's visit.

The dedication took place on July 16, 1988. A huge crowd—mountain people in great numbers, pilgrims, people drawn by the pope's return to the Adamello, families, the young and the not so young—waited for the pope in celebration. The arrival of the helicopter with the pope was a moment of great emotion for us. At the lodge, we had set up a sacristy in the garage where we kept the snowcat. We accompanied the pope there, he put on the sacred vestments, and we went to the altar for the Eucharistic celebration. The Mass was solemn and beautiful. He was wearing a white windbreaker that Franco and I had given to him, with the seal of the Italian School of Skiing on it: that day, we endowed him with the title of skiing instructor. His eyes were shining with happiness, and he seemed not to feel the cold or the wind. He remained standing for quite some time, seeming not to feel discomfort or weariness. Something was happening that engaged him deeply and completely. The words of his homily were so beautiful and intense that it is certainly worthwhile to recall them here:

> It is a great joy for me to be able to lift up to the Lord, together with you, the canticle of praise and gratitude here close to the summit of the Adamello, in front of the majestic glaciers of the Pian di Neve. Here, where nature is a perennial hymn to the greatness of the creator, it is easy to set our minds on lofty and invigorating thoughts, and to pause in prayer. The mountains have always held a special fascination for my heart: they invite us to climb not only materially, but also spiritually toward the realities that do not fade. Here, among the boundless spaces and in the solemn silence of the peaks, one senses the presence of the infinite! In this majestic and powerful scenery, man feels small and fragile, and more easily perceives the magnificence and omnipotence of God, the creator of the universe and the redeemer of the human race.

Here it truly happens that thought, in contemplating creation and even penetrating into the wonderful order of the entire universe, becomes a prayer of adoration and of trustful abandonment: "Lord, I believe in you, I adore you, I love you, and I hope in you!" Here around the altar of sacrifice, our thoughts go up to the salvific plan of the incarnation of the Word and of the redemption of man by means of his passion and death on the cross. On these immaculate heights, as we renew the sacrifice of the cross, we find ourselves really united with Christ the Lord, who has loved us and given himself for us. "Mountains and hills, bless the Lord, praise and exalt him above all forever" (Daniel 3:75).

From these mountains, one looks down to the surrounding valleys, and one's thought goes out spiritually to the people who populate them: women and men marked by the strong character of the mountain virtues. To them as well are addressed my greeting and blessing, with the hope that they may be faithful to the traditions that distinguish them: traditions of robust faith and of upright moral customs. I lift up my prayer that they not allow themselves to be overtaken by the temptations of consumerist society, by hedonism, by indifference, that they may look to the summits not only as the goal of their difficult daily lives, but also as a symbol of possible, uplifting, purifying spiritual ascesis.

The Mass celebrated on this altar, placed precisely where the front of the war ran in 1915–1918, is also a reminder and a prayer for the repose of all the combatants who, seventy years ago, on these harsh alpine crags, were wounded or went to meet death, invoking peace. As is known, this landscape, so serene and uplifting now, was the theater of terrible battles. Thinking of the harsh episodes of war that happened in these places, and of the countless victims mortally wounded in the gorges of these mountains, overcome by hatred and violence, one feels profound anguish for the fate of these men, at the mercy of the cruel vicissitudes of history. But we must also remember that in the immense amphitheater of these glaciers and these peaks, among which one can still see trenches and barbed wire, grenade fragments and the remains of wartime materials, although in strident contrast with the claims of nations, on both sides was present the comfort and friendship of Christ, the redeemer, who abandons no one and who loves all and wishes to save them for the life beyond time and history. How many times has the whiteness of the snow been stained red with blood! Our thoughts go out to all those who have fallen on the Adamello, to all the victims of wars past and present, to their families, to their broken dreams, and as we lift up our prayer for their repose, let us express once again our longing for and our invocation of peace, fraternity, harmony among peoples and nations.

In the future may it be peace that guides the journey of humanity. The majestic peace of these mountains is a call to commit ourselves to building and supporting a society free from the slavery of war and of hatred. We do not desire only the peace that silences weapons—although without a doubt this is a great good in itself—but we also desire the inner peace of hearts, which is the fruit of an upright conscience, of the sense of justice and charity, and is founded on the universal fatherhood of God the creator, on friendship with Christ, the Son of God who became incarnate precisely to deliver us from evil and show us our supernatural destiny.

Finally, the last reflection that I wish to propose for you, dear alpine people, concerns the commemoration of Our Lady of Mount Carmel, whose liturgy we celebrate today, July 16. For your twenty-fifth pilgrimage to the Adamello you have chosen a truly Marian day, you have decided to raise up beside this altar the image of Our Lady of the Adamello, which I will gladly bless at the end of the Eucharistic celebration. I am delighted by this gesture, which fits so well into the context of the Marian year, and by your devotion to the Heavenly Mother, who in every place and at every time is close to each one of us with her love and protection. Always, but especially at this celebration, Mary Most Holy reminds us that the essential aim of life is eternal salvation, and assures us of her intercession for perseverance in faith and grace until the end of our earthly pilgrimage. The Virgin Mary, who "advanced in the journey of faith" from this mountain as well, will look with eyes of motherly kindness on the populations of the surrounding valleys, helping them to have a faith capable of confronting the challenges of our times. Look with love, O Virgin Mary, on the

> poor, the suffering, the young, who are the hope of tomorrow. Be maternally close to all persons, families, and nations. Come to the aid of the Christian people in their fight against evil. O clement, O loving, O sweet Virgin Mary!

And then, after the celebration of the Mass, the pope expressed his thanks in these words:

> Once again I would like to extend my heartfelt thanks for this invitation during the Marian year. It was the duty of the pope to return here, after having come once before as a skier. He had to come during this Marian year to celebrate the Eucharistic service here. There is no place more suitable for this sacrifice of Christ. A place, an environment of so many sacrifices of young lives, of young persons, of brothers fallen in the Lord. So many sacrifices. The sacrifice of Christ had to be celebrated, which reminds us of his death, which gives us life, which assures us of the victory of life in him and for us. This mystery had to be celebrated here, today, and I thank you for having invited me. And you have invited me for a day so dear to me, the feast of Our Lady of Mount Carmel. The Virgin Mother of the Mountains must be present—just as Saint Luke recalls that, after conceiving the divine Word in the Holy Spirit, she went to the mountains to visit her cousin Elizabeth, [so also] she must be present in the mountains. She went into the mountains, and into these mountains of her town of Judea. In these mountains she heard the words,

"Blessed are you who have believed." The words that guide us during the Marian year.

This image of the Blessed Mother must be the sign of her faith that guides us all, that guides the whole Church, all peoples, all persons. All the communities on the earthly pilgrimage, but a pilgrimage of faith that leads us to life, supernatural life. I thank you for this invitation to the mountains where during this Marian year we have been able to celebrate what I would like to call the Virgin of the Mountains. It was in the mountains, in the home of Elizabeth, that Mary said the Magnificat. And this inspires us always, it inspires us together with the faith of Mary. And the word of nature, the grandeur of the mountains inspires us to repeat, "Magnificat." The Lord has done great things for us. I wish for you, dearest brothers and sisters, this Marian inspiration during the Marian year and all years. I wish it above all for you, dearest alpine people. I also wish for all mountain climbers and all skiers, for all inhabitants of the mountains, for all people of the mountains, for all those who love the mountains, that the mountains may always be for us the sign of the pilgrimage that leads above, that leads us to God. With these wishes I thank you once again, I leave you returning not on foot, not with skis, but in a helicopter. Praised be Jesus Christ!

Those hours were truly dense with great emotions for many people. Together with his usual charisma, John Paul II brought an emotional participation that could be clearly felt in the words he chose for the homily. What a strange effect, to see so much solemn intensity in the parts of the Mass in such an unusual context: the expanse of ice and that figure, white against white, priestly, with an expression of participation and suffering in the celebration of that mystery in a place that reechoes the sufferings of a long-ago and yet still tangible past.

There is one photo that, better than any words, sums up and symbolizes all of this: that of the pope lifting up above the pure white snow a consecrated host of equal whiteness. It is enough to look at his face, at the intensity of his expression, to understand the importance of such an emblematic gesture. And that significance did not escape those present. Once again a surreal silence had descended around him, a silence filled only with the rapid beating of hearts. After the ceremony, there was a private luncheon at the lodge. It was a simple and tasty meal prepared by Mamma Carla and spread out on a checkered tablecloth, and enjoyed with the rustic cheerfulness of us mountain people. How happy the pope was that day! At a certain point, he asked if he could go rest in the little room he had stayed in before. A short time earlier he had spent a few minutes absorbed in silence out on the terrace, looking straight in front of him at Cresta Croce . . . at the cross!

There is another beautiful photo that also bears witness to this most important detail: the pope holding onto the railing of the terrace, and looking out in front of him.

He is alone, with his shoulders slightly bent, an intense expression on his face, while all the people around him are keeping a respectful distance. The photographer (the incisive Marshal Colombo, whom we have already met in this story and who has unfortunately passed away) wrote about the photo: "In that place where he had been years before, John Paul II wanted to remain, for a few minutes, alone with himself. As if he were in ecstasy, as he contemplated the Cresta della Croce."

There is another image that was not photographed, however, imprinted and fixed before my eyes. I am certain, in fact, that in the absolute quiet of that little room the pope prayed for a long time, looking at the wooden cross. He must have reflected intensely on what it had meant to find himself there four years earlier, to be able to see something from that angle, to be able to intuit first and then fully comprehend something that concerned him very, very closely. The kernel of the secret, of "his" secret, had been deposited in him, within his very soul. Now it was there, still well hidden, but clear. John Paul II had not come to that place by accident, but according to a higher, precise, unquestionable will.

* * * * *

> "Around the ninth hour Jesus cried out in a loud voice, 'Eli, Eli, lemà sabachtanì.' That is, 'My God, my God, why have you abandoned me?'" (Matthew 27:46)

The mystery of these words remains unfathomable for us human beings: why was the Son of God himself, at the moment of supreme trial, death on the cross, seized by such a human form of distress? The love of the Father and the love of the Son is an eternal image of adoration for us believers. But over the course of the centuries, how many people would be touched by the suffering of another, albeit different, "crucifixion"? How many saints, martyrs, those persecuted for the faith have had to overcome their distress and accept their fate? And at certain times in our lives, is there not a moment in which we feel "crucified" and struggle to give meaning to those trials, feeling a growing desire to rebel, to renounce that Father who we nonetheless know is capable of loving us so greatly?

I have a suspicion that has a great ring of truth to it: Karol Wojtyla was one of those chosen ones. His witness of faith was present every day of his pontificate and of his life, to repeat his salvific mission on the earth each day. It was his destiny to dedicate himself completely to fostering the conversion and salvation of millions of people. His whole life bears witness to this. But on that day, that May 13, 1981, in Saint Peter's Square, at the moment of the worst phase of his "Calvary," would not he too have said, "My God, my God, why have you abandoned me?"

And afterward, certain that by the will of God he had been destined for that terrible trial, and, by the will of the Virgin Mary—who had deflected the bullet of Ali

Agca—it had not been fatal, must he not have sought out, as any other man would have done, evidence that would finally allow him to say, "It was all in God's plan, and his will that I should recover!"?

I am not a theologian, I am not a churchman or an expert on doctrinal matters. But I have faith. And every person of faith will agree, after evaluating the facts, that the meaning of his path is clear. It passed along the forbidding paths of the Adamello, until it encountered that "cross of rough-hewn trunks."

Nothing was coincidence. Perhaps it is only now, after his beatification, that we have been allowed to understand a little bit more about the life of this future saint whose undeserving friend I was. Everyone remembers that May 13, 1981, the date of the terrible attack in Saint Peter's Square, coincides in an incredible way with the apparition of Our Lady of Fatima: the same day, month, and hour. The account of the events that followed the shooting, from the testimony of the physicians at the Policlinico Agostino Gemelli in Rome who admitted the critically injured pope is precise:

> The pope was taken by ambulance to the Gemelli very quickly, in about fifteen minutes. He was immediately declared to be in critical condition. Don Stanislao was asked to give him the sacrament of extreme unction. He was then taken immediately to the operating room. Professor Francesco Crucitti, an excellent surgeon, made an incision and found, as he

> later recounted, "Blood, a great deal of blood, there may have been three liters. We decided to clear away the blood first in order to close a severe hemorrhage that constituted an imminent and deadly threat. We then proceeded with the transfusions that made the surgery feasible."

Exploring the pope's abdomen, they found various lesions. Some of them had been caused by the fragmentation of the projectiles, others by their penetration. One nine millimeter bullet had wounded the index finger on his left hand, which he had placed against his chest, and which slightly altered the bullet's trajectory. A bullet also pierced his colon and injured his small intestine. In spite of the gravity of the attack and the delicacy of the operation, the pope showed himself to be of extremely strong constitution. Although the bullets had taken almost a zigzag course through his body, his vital organs were unharmed. All of this allowed the pope to make a very quick—I would say miraculous—recovery, and after just four days the physicians released him from intensive care so that he could finish his recovery in more tranquil surroundings.

One more small detail: the nun who was able to grab hold of Ali Agca, stopping him in Saint Peter's Square, was named Lucia.

Many times, in confidence, the Holy Father had referred to the attack, telling me that he believed the Virgin Mary had intervened miraculously. He often mentioned the fact that he could no longer eat as before, that he had to break up his meals and reduce the portions, so that his compromised intestine would not suffer too much. He added that this was not the only time the Virgin Mary had intervened to save him, and often told about how when he was young, on a couple of occasions, he had needed that "motherly" intervention. He said that he had been saved in this way from being deported to Germany by the Nazis, and had come away unharmed from a terrifying accident on February 29, 1944, when he was hit by a truck.

At the time of his second visit to the glacier, for the celebration of the Mass on the beautiful new granite altar built on Cresta Croce, the pope had a new and powerful awareness of the connection between what had happened in long-ago 1917 and what had happened to him seven years earlier in Saint Peter's Square. A thread bound those events together, and that slender thread, in its unraveling, had also wrapped around our summit of the Adamello. It was a thread held by the merciful hand of the Immaculate Conception. By his second visit to our mountain he "knew" something that I, like the rest of the world, did not. But all of this, for the moment, had to remain a secret. . . . It was the pope's secret.

As I have mentioned before, over the following summers the Holy Father went to spend his vacations in Trentino or Val d'Aosta. That meant no more skiing, but instead long walks in the woods, where he could be immersed in the serenity of nature, to restore himself, to pray, to see the people and mingle with his faithful, something he enjoyed so much.

I never saw John Paul II become annoyed by the fact that in some way he was constrained. Wherever he went, he always had to share himself and his moments of recreation with strangers. This was a problem for us who were around him, and above all for his security team. For him, however, it was an authentic joy to stop to talk with anyone who crossed his path, even in the middle of the woods. Men, women, young people, families, elderly, or children—he was always ready to make himself available, to say hello, to ask people questions, to show interest, to give a hug. But I did see him become annoyed, and even very angry, if for reasons of logistics or security someone was taken away from him too abruptly.

In those cases he would speak in Polish with Don Stanislao, evidently complaining of the fact that the reasonable expectation of greeting the pope had been denied to that person. Obviously there were serious reasons for caution on the part of the security service, fears that were well founded, especially in those years following the attack. But although he was aware that he might be an easy target for someone who might still want to harm him, the pope never showed any fear or reluctance when someone approached him.

"Be not afraid . . ."

For him these were not merely words, but an exercise

of openness and trust toward humanity, which serve as a great example. The pope demonstrated an infinite tenderness in the course of those walks through the forest, even toward the animals. He was truly happy when we saw an ibex or a chamois, something that happened often, especially in Val d'Aosta. He was fascinated by the relative calm with which those magnificent animals allowed themselves to be approached. I saw him become very excited when this happened; he always preserved that sense of wonder, like that of a child who does not take creation for granted. He nourished the same insatiable curiosity for my expeditions, my far-ranging voyages. My ascents of the highest mountains in the world.

I knew that in some way, it was as if I could take him with me, carry his spirit in the bottom of my backpack. I am certain of this—in certain hazardous areas, in the farthest latitudes, I brought him along with me. I was walking with his legs as well, because his memory, his spirit, never left me. I understood this from the twinkling of his eyes when I went to say goodbye before each departure. Before I left on one of my expeditions, he invariably had me tell him the whole plan in every detail, including the difficulties and dangers. But never, even in view of the most dangerous plans, did he try to dissuade me or show any fear. He would simply bless me and give me a cross, smiling kindly. And I would leave with that smile firmly stamped in my mind. In the hardest moments, above all on certain terrible nights that seemed they would never end, I would think back on that smile and recover my energy.

It was this way in the spring of 1990. I went to Rome to say goodbye before an expedition to climb Everest, the legendary rooftop of the world at 29,029 feet. As usual, he became excited, displaying all of his emotional power. He blessed me and gave me a beautiful and finely detailed silver cross.

There were eight of us. We were all excellent climbers, a well-knit and highly motivated group, but when we arrived in Kathmandu we met with a nasty surprise: because of the disorganization created by the political conflict between the Tibetans and the Chinese, the border with the Tibetan side of the mountain, the one from which we were to begin our climb, had been closed.

The situation was not resolved, and the local agency that had organized the trip offered us an alternative: to scale another mountain of more than eight thousand meters, Dhaulagiri.

The "White Mountain," as its name means in Sanskrit, is part of the Himalayan chain. It is located in Nepal, and it is 26,795 feet high. It was discovered in 1800, and for about thirty years, until the discovery of Kangchenjunga, it was believed to be the tallest mountain on earth. Many people have lost their lives trying to climb it, including seven American climbers in 1969, six Japanese climbers in 1975, and four more Japanese in 1978. Shortly after I went on an expedition there in

1998, a famous French climber, Chantal Mauduit, was killed in an avalanche. Chantal was a wonderful woman: young, very pretty, cultured. Six times she had scaled peaks of more than eight thousand meters alone and without supplemental oxygen. She wrote a famous book entitled *I Live in Heaven*. Her spiritual testament in the words she has left us represent an admonition for us all: Be always ready for the challenges, those inside of us even before those of nature.

> No life is independent—even if the spirit roams through words, the beautiful, space, it does not walk, it does not fly except to reenter within itself in the whole, the one, alleviated of its earthly ego. Hermits in bodies imbued with the everyday, we delight in revisiting Himalayan bastions already delved, touching the ephemeral, gliding on the horizon, evaporating time in words taken from the feathers of a passing bird. Is not the essence of life, perhaps, to touch the sublime?

To touch the sublime . . . maybe that is what all those who make such unusual choices are seeking. The pope did so as well, by seeking out the highest spiritual summits, much higher than our own. Ultimately he and I always knew that ascending the rocky flanks of a mountain is a bit like walking in a holy place. This is why, in a strange way, he felt a sort of kinship with me, and out of empathy wondered what I was looking for up there, always higher and higher on the peaks.

I can still see myself at base camp, at an elevation of about sixteen thousand feet. The tents were pitched, including the mess tent complete with tables and chairs. It is there that people like me, who climb without oxygen tanks, get our indispensable acclimatization, which means getting the body used to higher and higher altitudes.

The first climb usually ends at an altitude of around eighteen thousand feet: there the first advanced base camp is built, a new little habitat that will constitute the new base of departure. Then the climber goes back down to the main base camp and rests for a few days before going up a little bit higher, always leaving from more advanced points: camp 2, then 3, 4, 5. It generally takes four intermediate camps to climb a mountain of eight thousand meters, and twenty or thirty days before making the final push to the top. Everything must be done while rationing one's strength, because it becomes increasingly difficult to breathe—when one inhales, it is as if the air cannot enter. Little by little, as one gradually climbs, every vital function slows down, it is as if the body suddenly becomes older and weaker, losing its muscular, cardiovascular, and respiratory power as the air becomes thinner.

In this sense, I have always had something of an advantage—living above ten thousand feet for many months of the year, I have always enjoyed a much higher level of blood oxygenation, and so I feel the stress of the altitude, which is no small thing, much less than my companions do. There is a moment at the beginning of any undertaking of this kind when one has a flash of mysterious clairvoyance, a touch of extra wisdom, which in some way is able to give you an impression of how things will go. I remember that on that occasion, at Dhaulagiri, I felt a vague unease, a sense of negativity. But in those moments one is unable to give this impression a name, and does not pay much attention to it. We made fairly rapid progress for at least the first two weeks. The weather was good, the temperatures not prohibitive.

Between camps 2 and 3—at an altitude of around 22,000 feet—it snowed constantly for three days. We decided that out of the eight of us, four, including me, would go on for the final approach. We were the ones who felt the best physically, but the difficulties were enormous. It had suddenly turned very warm after the storm, and we had to put on short-sleeved shirts. There was a wall of ice that was showing signs of crumbling.

We were walking on six feet of snow, very cautiously, because during a brief exploration the day before we had seen that many crevasses had opened. After a steep ascent we had already arrived on the last level stretch before the summit of Dhaulagiri. For the eyes and for the other senses, it is an unforgettable spectacle: the horizon becomes a boundary that embraces you. You feel like part of a whole, an element of that supreme beauty. We were taking turns "cutting" the snow, a few meters at a time, replacing each other very quickly because no one could make much headway without running out of breath. In our jargon, the one who "cuts" the snow is the one in the lead, the trailblazer. I was at the rear, and since I was about to replace the lead man, I sat down to catch my breath. In a flash I felt the "bridge"—the layer of ice covering a crevasse—collapse beneath me. I shot down immediately, disappearing from the view of the others. I was in darkness, bouncing back and forth against the icy walls of the chasm, swallowed up by the mountain fissure. I hit a layer of ice about fifteen feet down, breaking several ribs and splitting my chin open, but it also broke the deadly fall, sending me sliding down a small side channel.

From there I again tumbled down to the brink of the real precipice, which must have been a drop of several hundred yards. I landed on another "bridge" of ice, this time on my back, so that my backpack cushioned the fall. It had my sleeping bag in it, a thin mattress to insulate me from the ground, food and water. And, naturally, the cross. It is true that, in those few seconds, in those desperate straits, one's life really flashes before one's eyes. Then I simply thought, "That's it, just another moment and I'm dead!"

Instead, I found that I was covered with blood, and I felt an agonizing pain in my chest. I was injured, but miraculously alive. I heard the voices of my companions calling out to me and was able to respond, and then I saw that a rope had been lowered down for me. I realized that I had also broken a finger, but other than that I was able to use my hands. I grabbed the rope, attaching the carabiner at the end to the harness around my waist. I had to call on all my strength. I clenched my teeth and scrunched my eyes like a baby being born.

I wriggled out of a womb made for death, and won back my life. I was gushing blood, but I was alive—by a miracle! My body shook like a leaf with violent tremors. My companions realized that the gash on my face was very deep, but had not opened any major blood vessels; a few centimeters more and it would have severed my jugular. They bandaged it the best they could and two of them got ready to rush me down to base camp. One of the group was charged with going on, with finding the strength necessary to go forward. It was to him that I handed over the cross. I remember my hand shaking as I gave it to him, saying, "This saved me, take it up there."

I arrived back at base camp as if in a dream. One of our group, Claudio, had a wife who was a surgeon, and she had them put me on the table in the mess tent. She plastered my ribs and stitched me up with no anesthesia. Of course, I wasn't left with a lovely embroidery on my face. Let's just say that when I happen to touch this hard patch of skin, I say to myself, "It's great to be here still!" After this they took me to Kathmandu, and in a few hours the news traveled all over the world: "The pope's skiing instructor falls into a crevasse and is miraculously saved."

My parents learned what had happened, and desperately started trying to find out more. Through a telegraph, I was able to say that I was doing okay and that I was coming back to Italy. While my companions were still climbing to the summit, they found out that the border with Tibet had been reopened, so they decided to turn back and try to climb Everest, which had been our original plan. They brought the cross back with them, knowing that I had promised the pope to plant it on the rooftop of the world. But when they arrived at the advanced base camp on Everest it was already late in the climbing season, well into the month of June, with the storms already starting in the valley and the most prohibitive storms beginning at high altitude. At that base camp, at an altitude of 21,300 feet, the Italian climbers met the members of a Polish expedition, five highly motivated young men. They left together for one of the intermediate climbs, but got stuck for two days and two nights, fighting to keep their tents from being blown away in a powerful storm. At those temperatures, losing their tents would have meant certain death.

The Italians made it back down, but the five Poles did not. They got caught in an avalanche and died. That cross is still at the base camp, in a little niche carved into the rock. Beside it is a marble plaque with the names of the five young Polish climbers. Back in Italy, I was hospitalized for a few days and underwent a series of tests. In the meantime, my companions also returned, and we got together to console each other over our disappointment at the failure of the expedition. But as we analyzed the situation, we realized that we still had something to be happy about: we were all still alive.

As soon as I got out of the hospital, I wanted to take them with me to see the Holy Father, who naturally had already been informed of everything. I remember how pained he was to listen to the story of my mishap and of the tragedy of his fellow countrymen. He was deeply moved, and he took me aside and said, "You see, Lino, the Lord wanted to save you."

I added, in a whisper, "And you, Your Holiness, you must have put in a good word with your Boss!"

The physicians at the hospital examined the good work their colleague had done in an emergency situation and made one recommendation: they told me I should go spend some time near the ocean. Living at high altitudes together with the stress of such a terrifying accident had weakened my system, even though I appeared to be doing fine. In reality, I had some symptoms of altitude sickness: problems with my muscles, blood pressure, and lung function. At last I acknowledged that I would have to betray my beloved mountains for a while, in favor of the enchanting enticement of the sea. It was supposed to be just a short stay in a seaside location, and instead I was on the high seas for three years. I embarked on a one-hundred-foot yacht, the kind that competes in the regattas: masts that reach up to the clouds, pure speed and luxury. In other words, a world completely different from my own. These were toys in the hands of men like Raoul Gardini, Gianni Varasi, and Spanish king Juan Carlos. I have wonderful memories of this time, and it was certainly a more carefree life than the one I had led before and would resume immediately afterward. It was a respite, but nothing more.

On the boat, they called me the "mountaineer." I quickly learned to do my job, but it was perfectly clear that it was not my "cup of tea." If I had to say what binds me to the mountain with an exclusive and definitive love, other than the fact that I was born there, it is the silence. On the ocean there is always noise—the lapping of the waves, the slap of the rigging, the cry of the seagulls, the voices of the others packed into close quarters. In the mountains, in the most absolute silence, there is room for a voice that comes from within you, that all of a sudden makes you come to grips with yourself, with your life. And that voice sounds very much like that of God.

That voice, that sound amid the silence is something simple but very deep that connected me for twenty-one years to another "mountaineer," a pope and saint, but a "mountaineer" all the same. Every time I came back to land, even in those three years of "defection from the peaks," I would go to visit him in Rome. He would always receive me after Mass, and have me stay for breakfast. Those moments he was able to share with the people closest to him were his most joyful times. I remember how his eyes lit up with emotion when he saw me. Right away he called me by my name, "Lino, Lino, how are you?"

He never forgot to ask me for detailed news: about Mom first of all, then about my dad Martino, Franco, my sisters, and the children. Incredibly, he always remembered everyone, and showed a sign of affectionate interest in everyone. He certainly had a prodigious memory, in addition to demonstrating a beautiful sense of emotional closeness.

* * * * *

When I was thirty-two I met Giovanna, a woman with whom an unexpected passion erupted. She was already married, but the relationship was in crisis. It began playfully, like a game, but fate wanted to join us in the most profound way possible: with the arrival of a daughter. It was not an easy time, for me or her. Giovanna already had two little girls from her marriage, and we suddenly found ourselves facing an enormous responsibility. She was still living with her husband, and we had to make a decision quickly: to keep the child, or not.

I was a man accustomed to absolute freedom—I had my traveling, skiing lessons in winter and summer, my ambitious mountain climbing, and all in all I was really very afraid. It was not easy to accept the idea of taking on not only my responsibility as the father of one child, but a life with three of them. I don't deny that I thought intensely of my very special friend—he was my spiritual compass, almost a father figure. I couldn't lie to him. . . . I would have had to admit that I had committed that most horrible sin: not allowing one's child to be born. I thought about it for just a few hours, then I said to Giovanna, "Let's keep this child, and don't worry, I'll try to get used to the idea of having a pretty big family right away." The child was a girl, my beautiful Camilla. And her birth was my greatest joy. The first chance I got, I told the Holy Father that I was going to have a daughter, and with great affection and kindness he told me that this was exactly what he would have expected of me.

He encouraged me, saying that he was very optimistic, certain that I would also be able to love the other two girls sincerely. And he was right. It was the start of a life together that would last for seventeen years.

When the time came, the pope took my baby daughter into his arms with great joy. Unfortunately, we could not get married, because Giovanna was facing a long legal process to obtain a contentious divorce. Then, with the passing of the years, we found ourselves bitterly considering the fact that there was uncertainty on both sides, and our initial happiness seemed to have decreased. We had started to have problems in our relationship, and thought that staying together for life with sincerity would have taken an unnatural effort. And in fact, we never took that step. Until very recently, I was in what both Church and state consider a common-law marriage. In this regard, I think back on the many conversations I had with the pope, in private and in various circumstances, on issues like marriage, abortion, chastity, the indissolubility of marriage, or the obligation of the priest to renounce earthly love and family life.

As everyone knows, Pope John Paul II was very loyal to the orthodoxy of the Holy Roman Church. His books and the encyclicals speak to us of his desire to urge all the faithful to live authentically Christian lives, without giving in to the desire for modernity and superficiality.

He truly was a "good shepherd," capable of understanding and giving advice with kindness instead of judging. I believe that this is why he was a pope so loved by the people, charitable also in welcoming the lost sheep, forgiving and absolving. But he never stopped pointing out the right path, even for a moment.

I am reminded of the words of one of his speeches at a meeting with the young people of Turin on March 9, 1988. It was a speech that impressed me deeply because of his ability to enter into their hearts. The young—his strength, his recurring thought, those millions of young people all over the world who wanted to meet him—were truly his favorite audience. It is a pleasure for me to recall those words:

> What does it mean to love? One of you asks me,

"In your judgment, what does it mean for us young people to love?" I wanted to address these questions together with others, more complex, in which I have found your unease with exaggerated hedonism, widespread pornography, a permissive mentality, which fatally lead to "forgetting the highest and most indispensable values." So then, I agree with you: to love authentically as Christians today often means going against the grain, being straightforward people who call evil evil and good good, and courageously decide against the common practice of equating love with sex, validity with success, authenticity with appearance. To love as Christians is this miracle: to center ourselves on God through the person of Christ, and give ourselves to others in an attitude of openness, of welcome, of assistance. Within this context, vocations to marriage, as to consecrated life, will be vocations to love. By loving seriously, you will acquire the understanding and culture of love, correctness in seeing the demands and concreteness of self-donation. I confess to you in simplicity that I feel real disturbance over the future of the world, when I see young generations incapable of real love, or who reduce their self-donation to the exchange of gratification between equals, incapable of seeing sexuality as a call, an invitation to a higher and more universal form of love.

I believe that these words, in spite of the passing of time, are still relevant, and in fact never before has there been such a need to take this appeal into consideration.

In February of 1994, I went to the Vatican with my sister Miriam to visit the Holy Father and tell him about my departure on a new expedition to Everest. I wanted to bring to completion the enterprise that had failed a few years before. Once again, and with the same intense participation, he gave me a blessed cross. Two years earlier, he had a tumor the size of an orange removed from his large intestine, and the physicians said if it had not been identified it would have become malignant. But he looked like he was in good shape that day, and when we said goodbye I told him, "Your Holiness, as soon as I get back we'll go skiing."

"Gladly, Lino, maybe back on our beloved Adamello."

I left for the Himalayas at the beginning of spring, with the head of the expedition Giuliano De Marchi, an expert climber and a dear friend. He had also made an unsuccessful attempt to climb to the roof of the world.

We were both highly motivated to do everything we could to complete the expedition. We resumed with the usual tactics of approaching the giant. After the initial approach, we came to camp 6, at 27,000 feet, at about four in the afternoon. It was too late, and we were too tired, to make the final push and arrive at the last stage, about 28,000 feet. We realized that we were taking a big risk: being surprised by nightfall outside of the tents means certain death. One simply cannot survive temperatures of fifty degrees below zero.

In the tents, one sleeps in clothes and boots, and even

inside the temperature is very low, hovering around zero. It's bizarre to wake up in the morning with a big white icy mustache between your nose and mouth. Giuliano was close behind me when we decided to go back down to take shelter. We came to our agreement by shouting as is the usual practice, entrusting the words to the echo of the mountain. I arrived at the tent first, and ducked inside right away: I was exhausted. Before I knew it I dozed off, overcome by weariness and by the relative warmth.

It seemed to me that I slept for just five minutes, but when I woke up I realized that two hours had gone by. Giuliano wasn't there—strangely he hadn't come back. I went to go see where he might be, and I ran into an American climber and asked him to help me look for him. We found him in a pre-comatose state, and were just in time to save him from the worst. We carried him down to the tent to revive him, but I realized that he was getting frostbite in his hands and feet. I had to do all I could to warm him up to keep him alive.

When the night was over I understood that we had reached the end of our journey: I had to try to get him back down the mountain. I set out, dragging him behind me with the strength of desperation. The best-equipped base camp was further down, at an altitude of 20,000 feet, and it took us three days to get there. After they gave him some initial intravenous medication, we realized that some of his fingers and toes would need to be partially amputated. His condition was rather critical, and we decided to call off the expedition and hurry back to Italy. The cross remained in my backpack, but once again we had come back with the most precious gift: life. My friend Giuliano would meet his fate later.

He died a few years ago, after falling into a ravine during an expedition in Italy. It is still sad to think about it. And I think about it often. I try to console myself by telling myself that he died doing what he loved most. His last breath had left him there, among his mountains, in his own world.

Upon returning to Italy from Everest, I learned that the Holy Father had fallen in his bathroom at the Vatican and had broken his right femur. He was hospitalized at the Policlinico Gemelli for hip replacement surgery.

I cried. It seemed so awful to know that I would never be able to ski with him again. When I next saw him, he was using a cane, but he greeted me with the same smile as always. Neither of us had the courage to talk about skiing, neither wanted to upset the other. I told him only that I had decided to stop doing climbs of over eight thousand meters. They were too dangerous. I had Camilla now, and I should take fewer risks and stay closer to her.

As everyone knows, illness and suffering marked the pope's life in a dramatic way. So many surgeries, so many painful disorders, the deterioration of a physique that had been full of vigor, until the drama of the last period of his life, undermined by the terrible impact of Parkinson's, which he jokingly called "Mister P."

Everyone remembers the images of his physical distress during the dramatic last years of his life. But few remember what an example of courage he was for all of us. Whenever I could, I would attend his Mass for the World Day of the Sick, on February 11 of each year. On those occasions I observed something that escaped my understanding. It happened before my eyes but exceeded my rational and logical perception. He approached some of the sick with a different state of mind. In evaluating the suffering person in front of him, he seemed to be following a code entirely his own, like a radiologist who is able to diagnose a condition through the parameters of his own exclusive expertise.

He would mysteriously "select" some sick people, often those in whose anguished eyes he perceived some special pain or suffering. He tried not only to transmit hope and courage to them, but also to fill them with a deep sense of participation in a shared suffering. Today I feel able to say that his criterion escaped the perceptions of a "normal" person. I have become convinced that there was something different: in my opinion, this was one of his charismatic gifts, the exercise of a sort of foreknowledge, perhaps connected to the imminent death of those people. All those who, like me, have witnessed so many of those touching encounters with a truly suffering humanity, are likely to come to the same conclusion after careful thought. He was always powerfully drawn to the value of suffering, something that his own life would impose on him in such a profound way. I recall with particular emotion the message given by Pope John Paul II for the fourth World Day of the Sick, on October 11, 1995:

> "Do not worry about this illness or about any other misfortune. Am I, your Mother, not here at your side? Are you not protected by my shadow? Am I not your safety?" The humble Indian, Juan Diego of Cuautilan, heard these words on the lips of the Blessed Virgin, in December 1531, at the foot of Tepeyac Hill, today called Guadalupe, after asking for the healing of a relative. . . . Dear brothers and sisters who experience suffering in a particular way, you are called to a special mission in the new evangelization and to find your inspiration in Mary, Mother of love and human pain. . . . The Mother of Jesus is the model and guide of this effective proclamation, since she "places herself between her Son and mankind in the reality of their wants, needs and sufferings. She puts herself 'in the middle', that is to say, she acts as a mediatrix not as an outsider, but in her position as mother. She knows that as such she can point out to her Son the needs of mankind, and in fact, she 'has the right' to do so. Her mediation is thus in the nature of intercession: Mary 'intercedes' for mankind. And that is not all. As a mother she also wishes the messianic power of her Son to be manifested, that

salvific power of his which is meant to help man in his misfortunes, to free him from the evil which in various forms and degrees weighs heavily upon his life" (*Redemptoris Mater*, n. 21). . . . Upon all the suffering and upon those who expend themselves in their service, I invoke the maternal support of Mary. May the Mother of Jesus, venerated for centuries in the famous shrine of Our Lady of Guadalupe, hear the cry of this great suffering, dry the tears of those in pain and be at the side of all the world's sick.

VI

# A CROSS OF GRANITE THAT TOUCHES THE SKY

IN SEPTEMBER of 1996, during a lunch among friends in Pinzolo for the International Alpine Solidarity Award, an audacious idea was born. That wooden cross, so dear to the pope and to all of us, should not be given over to its inevitable fate: to disappear. Poor humble cross, it had withstood the years and the inclement weather, but how much longer could it last? Sooner or later it would disappear.

While I was talking about this with my friends Marshal Luciano Colombo, Marcello Bedeschi, and Faustino Pedretti, we decided that we would carve a granite cross into the bare rock of the mountain. Something that, symbolically, would recall the sacrifice of the alpine soldiers, carved from the bones of the same earth that had buried them, and that, in some way, was also the emblem of the extraordinary presence of the pope on the glacier. We were immediately overcome with enthusiasm: Punta

Croce would have it's name changed, becoming Punta Giovanni Paolo II. All of this was much easier said than done. Placing a granite cross at a elevation of 10,754 feet was certainly not a simple task. First of all a committee was set up, and Faustino offered to make the cross, together with his brothers and his employees. The rest of us would take care of the organization. Naturally, we immediately went to Rome to tell Don Stanislao about it, and then the pope. We were supported by another ally of exceptional faith and determination: Cardinal Giovanni Battista Re.

Don Stanislao and Cardinal Battista Re were happy about the initiative, but the Holy Father truly seemed to be seized by an uncontainable joy. He was the one who suggested that the project should be put into the context of the celebrations for the Jubilee of 2000. The humble cross of the Adamello, which for almost a hundred years had kept a solitary watch over the "sleep" of the alpine soldiers fallen at its feet, elevated to the rank of a symbol for future generations. Its history and its image would constitute a true example for the whole world, and for all those who have not had and will never have the good fortune to go up there to that little paradise concealed in the reflection of the glaciers.

We had a strong desire to proceed, but the difficulties were incredible. First of all, getting the cross into place would be dangerous. Only a helicopter would be able to position it at the top, but that spot on the mountain would have to be leveled to make a landing pad. The competent authorities immediately refused to give permission: it was too risky an operation, since the air currents at that altitude could have caused the imposing granite monument to sway. No pilot with good judgment would agree to such a hazardous undertaking. With a heedlessness that still astonishes me to this day, we pushed forward: Faustino selected a team from among his workers, the most skillful stone masons of Val Rendena, and the project was begun. The cross was carved from a single block of granite and shaped with skillful chiseling.

We all worked in our free time, as volunteers, with a passion that never diminished. We were fighting a war—in the jungle of red tape. The environment minister was against the plan. The defense minister was strenuously opposed, communicating a stern "No," that to us was worse than a cold shower. In their view, the conditions were not in place for approving a plan to fly a military helicopter into that environment. Only stubborn faith drove us to ignore the warning. It was difficult to admit it, but the possibility of success was minimal, and the heartfelt participation of the pope, from whom we naturally hid the difficulties, represented an additional worry: we were in danger of crushing the pope's hopeful anticipation. Every time he saw me, during the two years it took to reach the goal, he never failed to ask me, "So, Lino, what can you tell me about our cross?"

It was the historic pilot Giorgio Del Farra who

changed the course of things, guaranteeing us his support and perhaps the bit of good luck that we needed. He explained to the young aviators that the ordeal, arduous but not impossible, would provide an opportunity for experimentation on technical problems that had never been explored. It was a legendary enterprise: at 7:00 pm on July 21, 1998, a twin-rotor CH 47C-817 helicopter of the first AVES regiment "Antares," 11th squadron ETM "Ercole," flew into the bright blue sky above Punta Croce. On board were Lieutenant Colonel Dario Zampieri, Captain Francesco Martinelli, the marshals Cosimo D'Attis, Luciano Cesarini, Francesco Cassano, and Bruno Mastrogregori, nicknamed "The Raven." With prodigious maneuvers, they placed on the summit of the crest, as if it were a butterfly, a cross ten feet tall and weighing over four tons. Our cries of joy shattered the silence of the mountain: we were, elated, drunk with happiness, weeping and shouting like cavemen, before the indifference of the glacier. On August 1, the cross was presented to thousands of people—tall, imposing, illuminated by a cone of light on a day of leaden clouds. Then followed the Holy Mass officiated by Giovanni "Gianni" Danzi, Stanislaw Rylko, and Giovanni Battista Re. From that day forward, Cresta Croce proudly became Punta Giovanni Paolo II, and the pope expressed all of his joy in a letter:

> "Glory to God in the highest of heavens, and peace on earth to the men whom he loves" (Luke 2:14). The cross extends its arms majestically, and clasps all in a perennial embrace of peace, an appeal and an invitation to draw upon spiritual values for the energy to build a more fraternal and united world, a society finally free from hatred and war. Cross of Christ, banner of peace that from its lofty mountain peaks calls us to turn our eyes to the sky, uniting history with the eternal, speak to the hearts of those who see you shining in the night, and make them feel that God is close to us and loves us. I accompany these sentiments with a special blessing . . .

To make room for the new, sometimes it is necessary to sacrifice the old. But in doing so, one must never forget. . . . And it was with a trembling heart that a man gathered up the old cross, the precious emblem of that long-hidden secret. In the tiny village of Carisolo, in the heart of Val Rendena, lives that man, a mountaineer. He has a long, white beard, and he seems able to handle real life for only a few hours a day, then you wait for him to go back into the cover of his woods to help his friends the elves. His name is Remigio Righi, he was a stone mason, and he worked feverishly for months doing the detail work on the cross. But he is also the one who guards a precious treasure. He gathered it up from the snow, freshly cut down, with the love with which one gathers up a newly felled tree that knows the secrets of your life and has known so many of the things of the world. He put that humble cross to rest in a room, in silence and shadow. It leans against a wall of the "house of the alpines," in the headquarters of the association where those men of few words and great heart meet for a little talk and maybe a little "snifter" with the guys. The cross is there, the witness to all it has seen: life, death, miracles, love, the hopes and dreams of poor men. It has seen the most ferocious hatred, and many years later a joyful reconciliation. It has borne everything.

It is perhaps for this reason, because it has absorbed so much life, so much suffering, and so much love, that it was chosen to be placed in a little "joyful mystery." The mute observer, but not indifferent, it has watched the footsteps of a man dressed in white, in a time that extended beyond time. Now it is ready to tell it all to other men. On one of its trunks, rough as cork, has been placed a cap of green cloth:

> On the cap, on the cap we wear, there's a long, there's a long black plume. And it serves us, and it serves us, as a flag on those mountains, on those mountains to go to war.

But no. On the left side of that cap there is no longer the black feather, in its place is a big hole. It was made by the ferocious explosion of a projectile of that "White War." The cap was spat out again by the glacier, but the poor alpine soldier was not. Remigio doesn't like to talk much, he will cross his arms and go up with you to look at that cross and at that cap. He will show it to you and be silent.

In front of it, even a prayer becomes a whisper to heaven. Words are too much. For many, many years, I too avoided superfluous words. I kept to myself the strongest emotions, the habits, the memories, the expressions, and the teachings of the pope. And it was only at the approach of the triumph of John Paul's beatification that I decided to recount, to rethink, to remember. To understand, and make understood, a little more about the life of this future saint.

In order to continue our story now we need to take a step backward. We need to return to 1981, the *annus horribilis* in which the pope suffered the attack in Saint Peter's Square, in the same month, on the same day, and at the same time as the first apparition of Our Lady of Fatima, as I have already mentioned. It was while he was at the Policlinico Gemelli that the pope, after getting through the aftermath of the surgery, began to reflect on that singular coincidence. May 13! Fatima! At that point he asked to read the third secret, kept in the secret archive of the Holy Office. Up until that point he knew only what all the faithful in the world knew about it.

The protagonists of the events of Fatima were the three little shepherds Lucia dos Santos, ten, and her cousins Jacinta and Francisco Marto, seven and nine respectively. Lucia was born on March 22, 1907, in Aljustrel, a hamlet on the outskirts of the city of Fatima, and was baptized two days later. Her parents, Antonio and Maria dos Santos, had six children. They lived humble lives as farmers and lived in a plain, humble home. Francisco was born on June 11, 1908, and his sister Jacinta on March 10, 1910. The Martos were also farmers and devout believers who lived modestly. The three children, as was the practice in their rural area at the time, worked with the sheep after school. In the spring of 1916, while they were playing, a light suddenly enveloped them and a strong wind began to blow. In the middle of the light a young man appeared and said to them, "Do not be afraid, I am the angel of peace. Pray with me."

In a later apparition the angel asked the children to offer constant prayers and sacrifices to God. The children asked, "How must we sacrifice ourselves?"

The angel replied, "Of all that you can, offer a sacrifice to the Lord. Above all, accept and bear with humility the sufferings that the Lord will send to you." In the third apparition, which took place in the fall of the same year, the angel invited them to say a new prayer to God:

> O Most Holy Trinity, Father, Son and Holy Spirit, I adore Thee profoundly. I offer Thee the most precious Body, Blood, Soul and Divinity of Jesus Christ present in all the tabernacles of the world, in reparation for the outrages, sacrileges and indifferences by which He is offended. By the infinite merits of the Sacred

> Heart of Jesus and the Immaculate Heart of Mary I beg the conversion of poor sinners.

Offering them the chalice and the host, he said:

> Take and drink the body and blood of Jesus Christ, horribly outraged by ungrateful men. Make reparation for their crimes and console your God.

On May 13, 1917, while the three shepherds were with the flock at the Cova da Iria (Irene's Cove), after two dazzling flashes of light there appeared a beautiful Lady, brighter than the sun, who in a kind voice said to them, "Do not be afraid. I do not mean you any harm."

Lucia asked, "From where do you come?"

"I come from heaven."

"And what do you want of me?"

"I have come to ask you to return here for six consecutive months, on the thirteenth day, at this same time. . . . Then I will tell you who I am and what I want. I will then return here a seventh time."

"And will I go to heaven too?" Lucia asked.

"Yes."

"And Jacinta?"

"Her as well."

"And Francisco?"

"Him as well, but he will have to say many rosaries."

Lucia then asked for news about two girls who had died: "Maria Das Neves [a friend of theirs who had died at the age of sixteen], is she already in heaven?"

"Yes, she is there."

"And Amelia [who died at the age of eighteen], is she already in heaven?"

"She will remain in Purgatory until the end of the world."

Lucia asked again, "Can you tell me if the war will end soon or if it will still last a long time?"

"I cannot tell you this yet, until I tell you what I want. Do you wish to offer yourselves to God, ready to bear all the sufferings that he many want to send to you, in reparation for the sins by which he is offended, and to obtain the conversion of sinners?"

"Yes, we do!"

"Then you will have to suffer much, but the grace of God will be your comfort."

Lucia further recounts:

> At the moment in which the Blessed Mother spoke these last words, she opened her hands for the first time, transmitting to us a light so intense, a sort of reflection that came out and penetrated our hearts and the deepest reaches of our souls, making us see ourselves in God, more clearly than we see ourselves in the best of mirrors. Then we suddenly fell to our knees and repeated, "Most Holy Trinity, I adore you. My God, I love you in the Most Holy Sacrament."

After a while the Blessed Mother added, "Recite the rosary every day for peace in the world and the end of the war."

Then she rose and disappeared into heaven. On June 13, the feast of Saint Anthony, the second apparition occurred. The Blessed Mother announced her presence with a flash of light. Lucia and her cousins ran to the oak tree near which she had appeared the previous time. The Lady appeared wearing a white garment, and with the rosary in her hand.

She said to Lucia, "I want to tell you to return here on the thirteenth of the next month, to continue reciting the rosary every day, and I also want you to learn to read, and I will then tell you what I desire."

Lucia asked for the healing of a sick person, and the Blessed Mother replied, "Let him convert, and he will be healed within the year!"

Lucia: "I would like to ask you to take us to heaven."

"Yes, I will take Jacinta and Francisco soon, but you will remain here for some time. Jesus wants to use you to make me known and loved. He wants to establish devotion to my Immaculate Heart in the world. To those who will practice it I promise salvation. These souls will be beloved of God, and like flowers they will be placed by me before his throne."

"Will I remain here alone?"

"No, my daughter. Do not be discouraged, I will never abandon you. My Immaculate Heart will be your refuge, and the way that will lead you to God."

Several thousand people came on the following July 13. The news had gotten around. There was a sense of curiosity, but also of distrust and scorn for the children, whom some had judged as liars and braggers. At noon, announced by a flash of light, the Lady appeared.

"What do you want of me?" Lucia said.

"I want you to come here on the thirteenth of next month, and to continue saying the rosary every day to the Lady of the Rosary to obtain peace in the world and the end of the war, because only she can help you."

Lucia: "I would like to ask you to tell us who you are, to perform a miracle so that all may believe that you appear."

"Continue to come here every month. In October, I will say who I am, what I want, and I will perform a miracle that all will be able to see so that they may believe."

On that day the Blessed Mother entrusted to the children a secret made up of three parts. Lucia recounts:

> As Our Lady spoke these words she opened her hands once more, as she had during the two previous months. The rays of light seemed to penetrate the earth, and we saw as it were a sea of fire. Plunged in this fire were demons and souls in human form, like transparent burning embers, all blackened or burnished bronze, floating about in the conflagration, now raised into the air by the flames that issued from within themselves together with great clouds of smoke, now falling back on every side like sparks in huge fires, without weight or equilibrium, amid shrieks and groans of pain and despair, which

horrified us and made us tremble with fear (it must have been this sight which caused me to cry out, as people say they heard me do). The demons could be distinguished by their terrifying and repellant likeness to frightful and unknown animals, black and transparent like burning coals.

Terrified and as if to plead for succor, we looked up at Our Lady, who said to us, so kindly and so sadly: "You have seen hell, where the souls of poor sinners go. It is to save them that God wants to establish in the world devotion to my Immaculate Heart. If you do what I tell you, many souls will be saved, and there will be peace. This war will end, but if men do not refrain from offending God, another and more terrible war will begin during the pontificate of Pius XI. When you see a night that is lit by a strange and unknown light [this occurred on January 28, 1938], you will know it is the sign God gives you that He is about to punish the world with war and with hunger, and by the persecution of the Church and the Holy Father. To prevent this, I shall come to the world to ask that Russia be consecrated to my Immaculate Heart, and I shall ask that on the First Saturday of every month Communions of reparation be made in atonement for the sins of the world. If my wishes are fulfilled, Russia will be converted and there will be peace; if not, then Russia will spread her errors throughout the world, bringing new wars and persecution of the Church; the good will be martyred and the Holy Father will have much to suffer; certain nations will be annihilated. But in the

> end my Immaculate Heart will triumph. The Holy Father will consecrate Russia to me, and she will be converted, and the world will enjoy a period of peace. In Portugal the faith will always be preserved."

Then a vision followed in which the third part of the secret was given. Lucia describes it like this:

> After the two parts which I have already explained, at the left of Our Lady and a little above, we saw an Angel with a flaming sword in his left hand; flashing, it gave out flames that looked as though they would set the world on fire; but they died out in contact with the splendor that Our Lady radiated towards him from her right hand: pointing to the earth with his right hand, the Angel cried out in a loud voice: "Penance, Penance, Penance!" And we saw in an immense light that is God: "something similar to how people appear in a mirror when they pass in front of it" a Bishop dressed in White . . .

Do you remember the words from the beginning? All of this began in May of 1917. There would be another apparition, on the thirteenth of August, another on September 13, and again on October 13. The last of these, as the newspapers reported at the time, took place in front of an enormous crowd from the neighboring towns, but also from Lisbon, Oporto, and Coimbra. There were also journalists of the national and international press. It was estimated that there were 60,000 to 70,000 people at the event. Everyone was able to see what was called "the miracle of the sun." They saw the rain suddenly cease, the clouds open, the sun come out like a silver moon and spin dizzily, like a wheel of fire, projecting rays of light in all colors and in every direction. It lit up everything in the sky and on the ground, dazzling the immense crowd. After a moment's pause there was again a dance of lights, like a shining and richly colored pinwheel. There was another pause, and then, for the third time, a more colorful and brilliant fire than ever. The multitude of the people had the impression at certain moments that the sun had come loose from the sky and was falling to come burn up the earth. The enormous crowd shouted, "Miracle, miracle!"

The two youngest children, Jacinta and Francisco, as the Virgin Mary had predicted in one of her apparitions, died soon after. Francisco died on April 4, 1919, after a brief illness. Jacinta died of pleurisy on February 20, 1920, after contracting pneumonia in 1918. Lucia became a nun, joining the order of the Sisters of St. Dorothy, and on December 10, 1925, received an apparition of the Blessed Mother with the Child Jesus in her cell. The Blessed Mother showed her the Immaculate Heart crowned with thorns, and said:

> Look, my daughter, at my Heart crowned with thorns, which ungrateful men inflict on me at every moment with blasphemies and ingratitude. You, at least, seek to console me and assure all those who for five consecutive months, on the first Saturday

> of the month, confess with the intention of making reparation for the offenses against the Immaculate Heart, receive Holy Communion with the same intention, also on the first Saturday of the month, recite the Rosary, and keep me company for a quarter of an hour meditating on the fifteen mysteries of the Rosary with the intention of offering me reparation, that I promise that I will assist them in the hour of death with all the graces necessary for the salvation of their souls.

On October 3, 1934, Lucia took her solemn vows. On March 24, 1948, she entered the Carmelite convent of Saint Teresa in Coimbra, Portugal, and took the name of Maria Lucia of Jesus and the Immaculate Heart. Lucia, in her cell, received more apparitions of the Blessed Mother, who in 1927 told her that she could reveal the first two parts of the secret. Lucia set down in writing everything that she had seen and heard, and had it read by the bishop of Leiria (a Portuguese city halfway between Oporto and Lisbon), by her mother superior, and by two Jesuit priests. After obtaining permission, the first two parts of the secret were divulged in 1937.

Lucia wrote down the third part of the secret on January 3, 1944, in the convent of the Sisters of St. Dorothy in Tuy, in Spain, where she had been transferred. There was only one copy, and it was kept in a sealed envelope that was initially kept by the bishop of Leiria. In order to better protect the secret, on April 4,

1957, the envelope was delivered to the secret archive of the Holy Office. Sister Lucia was made aware of these decisions by her bishop.

On August 17, 1959, in agreement with Cardinal Alfredo Ottaviani, Fr. Pierre Paul Philippe, the commissioner of the Holy Office, brought Pope John XXIII the envelope containing the third part of the secret of Fatima. His Holiness, "after a bit of hesitation," said, "Let's wait. I will pray. I will let you know what I have decided." Pope John decided to send the sealed envelope back to the Holy Office, and not to reveal the third part of the secret.

On March 27, 1965, Paul VI read the contents together with Archbishop Angelo Dell'Acqua, and sent the envelope back to the secret archive of the Holy Office, with the decision not to publish the text. What would happen with Pope John Paul II?

On July 18, 1981, Cardinal Franjo Seper, the prefect of the congregation, sent Archbishop Eduardo Martínez Somalo, substitute at the Vatican secretariat of state, two envelopes: one of them was white, and contained the original text of Sister Lucia in Portuguese; the other was orange, and contained the Italian translation of the secret.

At that point, the pope found out and must have made his considerations with profound and thoughtful emotion. He must have reviewed the first two parts of the secret, considering that everything that had been predicted and announced to the shepherds by the Blessed Mother had come true. The first part concerned the confirmation of the existence of hell. The second part announced that the First World War was about to end, but that during the pontificate of Pius XI another would break out, even worse, "preceded by a night illuminated by an unknown light"; it then said that Russia would "spread its errors throughout the world, promoting wars and persecutions of the Church."

Everything seemed to have come true, including what was at first considered a mistake, since the Second World War was supposed to have broken out during the pontificate of Pius XI, according to the secret. Historians date the beginning of the conflict to September 1, 1939, when Pius XII was pope. But the message says that the catastrophe would be announced by "a night illuminated by an unknown light," and the night between January 24 and 25 was illuminated by an exceptional aurora borealis. Less than two months later, on the night between March 11 and 12, 1938, during the pontificate of Pius XI, German troops invaded Austria. Hitler had Chancellor Kurt Alois von Schuschnigg arrested, and on March 15 proclaimed the annexation of Austria to the Third Reich, beginning the most terrifying tragedy of the twentieth century.

What happened next is recent history. He was a pope from the East dramatically affected by the errors of Russia. That bishop dressed in white. On August 11, the pope gave the envelopes back to Cardinal Martínez Somalo, and they were again entrusted to the absolute secrecy of the Holy Office. So the pope knew, but he decided to keep quiet, and once again the third secret . . . remained secret.

What determined this decision? Perhaps it was his desire to understand more and better. It seemed that he was that bishop in white, but Saint Peter's Square is not a steep mountain, and in the middle of it is an Egyptian obelisk, not a cross of rough-hewn trunks. The city is not in ruins, no one has died, and he was certainly not shot by a group of soldiers.

On the other hand, it is also true that the attack mysteriously took place on the anniversary of the first apparition of Our Lady of Fatima, and that the pope himself was immediately convinced that the shots were deflected and his life saved by the Blessed Mother. So he did not speak, but he wanted to do something extraordinarily significant to thank her.

On May 13, 1982, one year after the attack, the pope went to Fatima, where, with an "act of entrustment," he said, "I consecrate and entrust to Mary the world, and in particular those men who are in particular need of this entrustment and this consecration." In front of the chapel of the apparitions, in the presence of the bishop of Leiria, Alberto Cosme do Amaral, he said,

> For a long time I had the intention of coming to Fatima; ever since the well-known attack in Saint

> Peter's Square, one year ago, when I regained consciousness my thoughts turned immediately to this shrine, to place in the heart of the heavenly Mother my thanks for saving me from danger. I saw in everything that was happening, and I will never tire of repeating it, a special form of maternal protection of the Blessed Mother. And in the coincidence—there are no mere coincidences in the plans of divine providence—I also saw an appeal, and perhaps a drawing of attention back to the message that went out from here sixty-five years ago, through three little ones, the children of humble rural people, the shepherds of Fatima.

With a gesture of incredible symbolic power, the pope then asked to have the bullet from Agca's gun placed in the crown of the statue of the Virgin. To everyone's surprise, it was not even necessary to make a place for it, because there was already a hole in the crown into which the bullet fit perfectly, as if it had been designed that way.

* * * * *

Time does not obey human haste; time is a river that flows and pulls things along according to the plans of God. The pope came to spend a very brief vacation in the place suggested to him by Don Stanislao and discovered a reality that must have penetrated within his heart, into the darkness of his blood, into his guts. Recall the words of the third secret of Fatima.

"And we saw in an immense light that is God . . ."

*The dazzling light that strikes the perennial snow; the dimension in which God is found the most.*

"Something similar to how people appear in a mirror . . ."

*The glaciers that reflect like mirrors.*

"Going up a steep mountain . . ."

*The steep summit of our mountain.*

"At the top of which there was a big Cross of rough-hewn trunks as of a cork-tree with the bark . . ."

*The cross, our beloved cross of rough-hewn trunks, eaten up, so eroded by the wind and by the ice that they resembled cork.*

"Before reaching there the Holy Father passed through a big city half in ruins . . ."

*"Lino, Lino, what was here"? Barracks, fortifications, a tower . . . it looks like a city half in ruins.*

"Afflicted with pain and sorrow, he prayed for the souls of the corpses he met on his way . . ."

*How many soldiers died here, Lino? Let's say a prayer.*

"Beneath the two arms of the Cross there were two Angels each with a crystal aspersorium in his hand, in which they gathered up the blood of the Martyrs and with it sprinkled the souls that were making their way to God."

*The ice was red with blood, Your Holiness, the souls of the soldiers were going back to God.*

Believing takes faith, but all it takes to love is to be born into this world. To hold together all the pieces of my memories of the pope, I used only the glue of love. That was simply my world. Someone had foreseen that he would come to us. And it is there that he recognized his destiny, I have become sure of it. He looked it square in the face, without fear. I think back on it now, I see it again: I see again the expression on his face, in that moment in which his mood would suddenly change. We were right beneath the "road of the alpines," we saw the rock wall with the soldiers' trenches, the wooden ladders, the traces of that sorrowful past, which came back in a flash.

Up there on the Adamello, I am sure of it, seated on that rock in recollection, God called him to report, tenderly laying a hand upon the pope's head. And, there on our mountains, the pope understood everything. He said once again, "Here I am, Lord, your will be done." The man then put his skis back on, and the saint went into hiding, once again submerged within his heart.

Someone, on a public occasion, had asked him one day, "Holy Father, what is sanctity?" He replied, "If one could gather all the light of the sun into one place, it would shine with dazzling splendor. But who can express the beauty of the soul of the one in whom God dwells? The saint is the happy collaboration of man with God, the author of all beauty. Lord, I have only one life to accomplish all of this!"

Now we know that one life was enough for him: on the evening of December 31, 1999, at the transition to the new millennium, the RAI (the official Italian television network) broadcast images depicting Cresta Croce at the express desire of the pope. It was his blessing *Urbi et Orbi*, in the sign of that cross, for millions and millions of people. An emblematic gesture, the meaning of which is clear today, like the words that he entrusted to Cardinal Angelo Sodano in a message he wrote for the occasion:

> With joy I have learned of the initiative to illuminate during the night of transition between this century and the next millennium the grandiose Cross of granite that stands on the Adamello. There, where during the years of the First World War the front line ran and so many human beings fell before their time, the light of the Cross of Christ will shine, a message of peace and reconciliation, of hope and solidarity, which will flood valleys and mountains.
>
> I express appreciation for this evocative initiative, keeping always in mind the two occasions on which I had the opportunity to spend a few hours on those snowy peaks in July of 1984 and of 1988. I still carry alive in my heart the emotions that I felt back then. In the context of the Jubilee year, the simple and eloquent gesture that is being performed constitutes a meaningful invitation to set our eyes on Christ and on the mystery of the cross that illuminates and gives meaning to the trials of human existence. May

> the light of the Cross of Christ, which from the Adamello will shine upon the valleys of Brescia and Trento, arrive even within the furthest houses, and just as the same light guided the shepherds to the cave of Bethlehem, so also may it lead all to encounter the Savior in the mystery of his love for us. In this Christmas season, the proclamation of the Angels echoes with particular intensity: "Peace on earth to the men whom God loves" (Luke 2:14).
>
> The cross extends its arms majestically, and clasps all in a perennial embrace of peace, an appeal and an invitation to draw upon spiritual values for the energy to build a more fraternal and united world, a society finally free from hatred and war. Cross of Christ, banner of peace that from its lofty mountain peaks calls us to turn our eyes to the sky, uniting history with the eternal, speak to the hearts of those who see you shining in the night, and make them feel that God is close to us and loves us. I accompany these sentiments with a special blessing, which I sincerely impart to you and to the Christian communities of Trento and Brescia.

The following morning, January 1, 2000, the pope would go to the Roman basilica of Saint Mary Major to open the Jubilee year.

VII

# PRAYING AT THE NORTH POLE

IN 2001, together with a great friend of mine, Mike Bongiorno, I set out on a great adventure: an expedition to the North Pole that sprang from an encounter we had with John Paul II.

I had met Mike almost twenty years earlier, and our friendship had been born thanks to our shared passion for sled dogs. In fact, we participated together in the first dogsled race in Italy. The mutual friendship was immediate and spontaneous: he, as passionate as I was about skiing and the mountains, wanted me to go with him on some expeditions. I knew that Mike had a desire hidden in his heart, as well: to be received by Pope John Paul II, a man he greatly admired.

Mike was a man of faith, but the fact that he had been divorced made an official encounter with the pope more difficult. I worked to let those closest to the Holy Father know how important this was to Mike, and in the end the permission was granted. I accompanied him to the Vatican myself, together with his wife Daniela and with their three children, Nicolò, Michele, and Leonardo. They were received in the papal apartment, early in the morning, for the Mass. Mike was so moved, his eyes were glistening.

Later, he would tell me, thanking me, "You have given me one of the happiest days of my life." He and the pope understood each other right away. Like real mountaineers, they started talking about skiing and about boots with crampons, because Mike had brought him a white pair of these as a gift. John Paul was moved as well. He knew he was in the presence of a man who had lived an extraordinary life, who had looked death in the face in a Nazi concentration camp.

The ceremony was supposed to be quick, but the pontiff and Mike did not want to separate. I still remember the sly look when Mike, jokingly, made an appointment with the pope to go skiing. And the pope, having recovered from the recent fracture of his femur, said with a touch of satisfaction, "Eh, the mountain has lost a great skier."

Then we told John Paul about the expedition to the North Pole. We had decided to schedule it for the centenary of the epic expedition conducted by Luigi Amedeo d'Aosta, duke of the Abruzzi. When we told him, the pope said, "You must take the cross to the North Pole, the cross of Jesus, to the farthest latitude." Mike and I promised that we would make that dream come true.

Before our departure, the pope blessed a truly special cross, made by the sculptor Andrea Trisciuzzi. On the central beam were represented various stylized figures, climbing up toward the crucified Jesus. As they got higher and higher, the suffering disappeared from their faces, giving way to smiles of hope. The last figure, at the top, was that of the pope: he was reaching up with one hand, and Jesus was reaching down to pull him up.

We were accompanied on the adventure by Monsignor Liberio Andreatta, who, as the pope wanted, celebrated Mass every day on altars improvised on the ice, while Mike and I acted as altar servers. We reached the North Pole on Easter, and planted the cross. But it was not possible to leave it there, because the glaciers were starting to melt, and who knows where it would have ended up. We doubled back to the Arctic Naval Museum of Saint Petersburg: in this way, the pope's cross brought its sign of Christianity to the most atheistic country in the world! My desire, now, is to plant a copy of that unique cross on the summit of an Italian mountain. Waiting together for the event with trepidation and joy are the pope and Mike, who passed away in September of 2009.

* * * * *

On April 27, 2000, Cardinal Tarcisio Bertone, the secretary of the congregation for the doctrine of the faith, entered the Carmelite convent of Saint Teresa in Coimbra, Portugal. He was accompanied by the bishop of Leiria, Serafim de Sousa Ferreira e Silva. Pope John Paul II had sent Bertone in great secrecy to meet with Sister Lucia. He found her lucid and serene, very happy to receive a letter of greeting from the Holy Father, who asked her to respond in all tranquility and frankness to the cardinal's questions. Sister Lucia said that she was honored to do so. Cardinal Bertone showed her the envelope containing the third secret of Fatima.

And Sister Lucia: "It is my letter, it is my writing."

Cardinal Bertone then asked: "Is the main figure in the vision the pope?"

Sister Lucia immediately answered, "Yes," and recalled that she and the other two shepherds were very sad about the pope's sufferings, and that Jacinta said repeatedly, "Poor Holy Father, he has so much pain on account of sinners!"

Sister Lucia continued, "We did not know the name of the pope, the Lady did not tell us the name of the pope, we did not know if it was Benedict XV or Pius XII or Paul VI or John Paul II, but it was the pope who was suffering, and seeing his pain made us suffer too."

The conversation ended with an exchange of rosaries: Sister Lucia was given one from the pope, and she presented a few that she had made with her own hands. Saying goodbye and imparting a blessing in the name of the Holy Father, Cardinal Bertone said, "I hope to see you again soon and in good health."

And she: "No, Your Excellency, you will not see me again alive. But you will come to bless me."

She was ninety-three years old, and she would live for four more years. In her last days, not having lost the gift of a subtle wit, she said, "The Blessed Mother said that I would remain here for some time, but so much has gone by!"

A few days after her meeting with Cardinal Bertone, she went back to Fatima for the supreme joy of the beatification of Francisco and Jacinta. There she met the Holy Father, and the two immediately developed an extraordinary affinity for each other and a spontaneous affection, which remained intact to the very end. They wrote to each other frequently, and anyone who saw them together could see that both of them were living in a supernatural dimension, endowed with the charismatic gifts proper to the saints.

In the homily of the Mass on that May 13, 2000 (the beatification of Jacinta and Francisco, and the nineteenth anniversary of the attack on John Paul), the pope cited Matthew: "I bless you, O Father, Lord of heaven and earth, because you have hidden these things from the wise and intelligent, and have revealed them to the simple:" (Matthew 11:25). On the return trip, the pope was very happy and kept repeating, "Finally I have done what I had to do. I have beatified Francisco and Jacinta."

Sister Lucia, who as a young woman had tended the

garden, been a teacher, embroidered, and done many other things, in her last days had been unable to use her legs. It was her fellow sister Maria Celina, who was very close to her, who recounted the end of her extraordinary life:

> When in the winter of 2004 her condition became more critical, John Paul II was advised, and sent her a message and his blessing. She was already rather ill, and asked me to have near her the statue of Our Lady of Fatima that had been given to her by the Holy Father himself. She brought it to her lips and kissed it. It was her last kiss! I read her the text of the pope's message, but she reached out her hand, she wanted to take the page, which she placed on her knees. She tried to speak, but was unable. Starting at midday on February 13, she began to "slip away." Her breathing became difficult. She continued to deteriorate, and in the afternoon Bishop Albino Cleto also came. The bishop began the prayers, all her fellow sisters were in the little cell. At a certain point, those eyes that had contemplated the invisible so many times opened again. She turned to her right and stared into my eyes. I cannot describe the profundity of that gaze. It was touching! I positioned the crucifix in the direction of her eyes. After this, she closed them again. It was her goodbye! It was the day 13 (that number again!) of 2005. Precisely 5:24 p.m. The three shepherds were reunited in heaven!

* * * * *

In 2003, with the approach of the twenty-fifth anniversary of his pontificate, John Paul II expressed the desire to have the first two medallions stamped for the occasion mounted at the foot of the monument erected on Cresta Croce. He had the bullet that had pierced his intestine placed in the crown of Our Lady of Fatima, the bloodstained white sash that he had been wearing on the day of the attack he gave to the Polish shrine of Jasna Góra, and he wanted the medallions of his pontificate to be placed in our granite cross on the Adamello. Is there not a logical connection running through all of this?

One of the medallions depicts the pope with one of his hands extended toward the Virgin and Child. And written there: *Joannes Paulus PP. Anno XXV Pontificatus.* The other shows Jesus raising his arm, and many souls drawing close to him: the one highest up is a soldier wearing a helmet, one of the many who fell up there. The inscription on this one represents another act of faith: the profession "I believe," shouted out to the world. It is taken from a passage of the Gospel of Matthew (16:16): "You are the Christ, the Son of the living God."

Immediately after the death of Lazarus, Jesus says to his sister, Martha: "I am the resurrection and the life; he who believes in me, even if he dies, will live, and whoever lives and believes in me will never die. Do you believe this?"

And she answers him, "Yes, Lord. I believe that you are the Christ, the Son of God, he who is to come into the world" (John 11:25–27).

* * * * *

In February of 2005, just two months before the pope passed away, Cardinal Bertone went back to Portugal. Exactly as Sister Lucia had predicted, he returned to bless her and to celebrate her funeral. Messages came from all over the world, and documents began to be collected immediately for the start of her cause of beatification. The pope's health had also been worsening gradually in recent years. In 2001 he was diagnosed with Parkinson's disease, and in 2003 the Vatican officially confirmed the news.

I often asked Don Stanislao for news about the drugs that were being prescribed for the pope. Every time his treatment was changed, he reacted well, he seemed to be doing better, the illness seemed to have retreated, but then . . . he started to get worse again. He never talked about this with me. He was reluctant to allow himself to be helped in even the most simple daily tasks: eating, getting dressed. He was proud and dignified. He faced suffering in silence, and without complaining.

A tender image is engraved in my mind from when we were in Les Combes in Introd, in Val d'Aosta. It was July of 2004, and the pope had not wanted to give up his usual vacation in the mountains. We had long since ruled out uphill trails, but by then we even had to keep him off level terrain if it was rocky or broken. We would take him in a jeep to a clearing, a peaceful and comfortable spot, and he contented himself with staying there in the quiet.

I see it again in my mind's eye: a bright green meadow, the sunshine of a long summer afternoon, and him alone, sitting with the breviary in his hands. An image of rare harmony, he seemed to be completely at one with his surroundings. It was to be his last summer, his last vacation.

During the Angelus at a local church, he had said on one of those days, "I thank God for the majestic beauty of creation. I thank him for his own beauty, of which the cosmos is like a reflection, capable of captivating attentive hearts and of moving them to praise his greatness."

* * * * *

In 2002, I had seen him happy as a child because of the success of an initiative that we set up at the Vatican. It was a special evening, an exception for him, who no longer went to performances because of his health. A *Hymn to the Peaks* had been composed, a beautiful piece of music, and I must say that we found a method of execution that was rather original. It was broadcast live worldwide, and while the orchestra was playing in the Sala

Nevi, the chorus sang its parts from the shrine of Monte Lussari, and the soprano from the Gran Sasso. It was full of beautiful sounds and images, and for the pope, brought great and heartfelt joy.

Two years before, something truly important had happened, an event that raised a commotion across the whole world.

After hearing about the confirmations provided for Cardinal Bertone by Sister Lucia, John Paul II made his decision: he would reveal the third secret to the world. The time had come. He felt there was no need for further investigation. The revelation was made public at a press conference in the austere Vatican press office, which had been decorated with ferns and yellow and white wild roses for the occasion.

It was June 26, 2000. The responsibility for telling the whole world about what had remained hidden for fifty-six years fell on the shoulders of Cardinal Joseph Ratzinger, the future Pope Benedict XVI. I always knew that there was a relationship of extraordinary trust between the two: they almost understood each other without speaking. So it was that John Paul II's successor oversaw the publication of a booklet entitled *The Message of Fatima*, accompanied by his own theological commentary.

It was Cardinal Ratzinger himself who declared, "It is a private revelation, no one is obliged to believe in the 'prophecy' of Fatima, which remains a 'private revelation,' but it is credible. The bishop dressed in the white who according to the secret is 'killed' is the pope: after the attack in 1981, he recognized himself in that figure, and maintains that he was saved by Our Lady, and I share the opinion of the pope."

During the press conference, which was broadcast live by Rai Uno and watched in more than forty countries, someone asked why it had taken so long for the secret to be made known. Cardinal Ratzinger, who at the time was the prefect of the Congregation for the Doctrine of the Faith, responded that before the attack, it "did not speak, it was not comprehensible." And that even afterward, "perhaps it was not the right time." To someone who pointed out the inconsistency between the pope of the secret (who was killed) and John Paul II (who was saved), Ratzinger replied: "The vision is not the film of an irremediably fixed future, it has a symbolic value and signals a threat, and tends to mobilize forces that can alter it."

Cardinal Ratzinger concluded, saying, "The decision of the Holy Father to make public the third part of the secret of Fatima closes a passage of history marked by the tragic human desire for power and iniquity, but permeated by the merciful love of God and by the attentive vigilance of the Mother of Jesus and of the Church."

Because of my position as director of the Foundation for the Mountain, I was in Rome much more often during the last years of the pope's life. I visited him regularly, and he always found a moment, however brief, to hear about what I was doing or to hear news about my family.

On the last Wednesday of January in 2005, at the general audience at the Vatican, I was there with my sister Miriam and a few friends, plus the members of some families that had been asking me for a long time if they could meet him. There was also little Luca, Miriam's son. The pope had baptized Luca, and he embraced the boy with the affection of a grandfather.

A few days later, on January 31, I went to Milan to visit some of the friends who had been with us at the Vatican. I wanted to take them the photos of us with the pope. I stayed for dinner and then went back to Val Camonica, where I live. I had almost arrived when I suddenly saw an oncoming car in my lane, skidding and coming right at me. I tried to swerve to avoid it, but it was no use. I remember my car turning over a couple of times, the screeching of the metal, and the sense of powerlessness as I perceived everything very clearly. In a moment, I then thought, "Maybe I'm already dead, and I just don't realize it."

My doubt was removed when someone stopped at the scene. In the darkness of the night, he called out to me, but I couldn't move, I was trapped inside the car. I heard him talking excitedly on the telephone, asking for help: "One driver died on the spot, the driver of the other car is still alive, but come quick, because he's in really bad shape." I drifted out of consciousness.

I woke up in intensive care. I had multiple fractures, and I had also hit my head. As soon as I felt a little better, the doctors told me that my chances of walking again were slim, and that to have any chance I would need to undergo a series of microsurgery operations. I was in a wheelchair for six months.

On that chaotic night, many miles away from me, something equally terrible happened, just half an hour after my accident. Pope John Paul II felt very ill and was rushed to the hospital. A long, terrible Calvary began which would soon require him to get a tracheotomy to allow him to breathe.

Once again his fate and mine had crossed paths. I found out almost immediately, and I wasn't very surprised. I thought that ultimately there is a very porous boundary between life and death, there are games that are played up there, heavenly battles with angels and demons, and down here we never know who wins. We are simply required to do our best: to adapt.

I remember with great sadness the days that followed: when for the first time in the twenty-six years of his pontificate he missed Ash Wednesday Mass. And March 27, Easter day, the first that he was unable to celebrate Mass. He came to the window and tried to speak, but was unable. I was at home on that evening of April 2, 2005, sitting on the couch. A few days earlier I had begun to take a few steps using crutches. My television was always on, waiting for that news. The days crawled by.

The news I never wanted to hear came that April 2, around ten o'clock at night: the pope, they announced, had gone back to the house of the Father. The whole world wept for him, in the grip of the deepest emotion. But not me. I didn't weep, I had only one thought: I had to go say goodbye, I had to get myself into shape to go to Rome. It wasn't easy. Pieces of steel were coming out of my toes, remnants of a series of operations that were healing my fractures. I don't know how I did it, but I did.

I arrived in Rome on the evening before the funeral, on April 7. Rome was under siege, a city shaken by the event. I went to the Vatican, where a blue car took me behind the basilica, to the side of the entrance reserved for heads of state and authorities. I saw the royal family of Spain get out of the car in front of me. I felt out of place: I was not a royal, I was just a "mountaineer," his "apostle of the mountains." Don Stanislao saw me and immediately came over to greet me. His eyes were shining, and he said to me emotionally, "Lino, once again John Paul II has saved you, I know it for sure."

Don Stanislao is not a man who wastes his words. He had confirmed what I already knew in my heart: "my friend" the pope had worked a miracle for me. As I left, I looked up to the skies of Rome, where clouds had appeared, taking on the reflections of many colors, and all of them streaked with gold: a magnificent spectacle, but I could not be consoled. The following morning, I was seated right behind the cardinals in Saint Peter's Square, and I had a clear view of the casket. They had placed it on a patterned rug. On either side were the Easter candle and a crucifix. Above the coffin was the Gospel, with the pages ruffled by a forceful wind that had been sweeping through Rome.

"The wind blows where it will, and you hear the sound of it, but you do not know from where it comes and where it goes: so it is for anyone who is born from the Spirit" (John 3:8).

It is to John Paul that I turn my thoughts: the wind symbolizes the Holy Spirit, and it was not blowing by coincidence that day. We all thought it. It was blowing for you. It was blowing because the Spirit of God was the source of your seven gifts: wisdom, understanding, counsel, fortitude, knowledge, piety, fear of the Lord. Actually, no. Not the last one, because you were never afraid of God, and that was why you told us to be not afraid.

As Cardinal Ratzinger celebrated Mass, in the piazza alone there were more than seventy thousand people, and an unreal silence. . . . Again that unique silence, your silence, the same as back then: "Lino, let's look for a peaceful spot. The Holy Father wants to be alone for a while." And everything was silent—the people, nature, the birds, and all things visible and invisible. On that day in Saint Peter's Square, the people recognized your silence, and respected it. In absolute fashion.

Through the silence a banner lifted up in the crowd,

with the words "*Santo subito*" ("sainthood now"), spoke for everyone. Seven years have gone by since then, and John Paul has been beatified. And my life has also gone forward, without him. I can't say that I have missed him, because he has always stayed with me, I have not let him go. He is with me, like every drop of my blood. If I have a problem, I talk to him about it, and I hear his voice answering me. I smile to think about how he will manage to answer everyone, because there are millions all over the world who are turning to him.

One of them was a French nun named Marie Simon-Pierre, and her inexplicable healing is attributed to the intercession of Pope John Paul II. Like him, she suffered from Parkinson's disease, but she is certainly not the only one to claim to have received a grace from him. There is a long list of testimonies, among the documents gathered by the postulator. The whole world now knows what we already knew: he is a saint.

* * * * *

"Lino, Lino, when are you going to get your head straight?" It now seems that I have done this "job." Three years ago I met Alba, the woman who suddenly made me understand why I had always run away from making a definitive decision. Because I was waiting for her!

In September of 2009, I took her to the altar in a little church where we live. Our wedding was officiated by

Cardinal Giovanni Battista Re, himself a proud mountaineer. For a Catholic, to say "forever" is an important value. Beside me, to hear that promise, in addition to the obligatory witnesses, there was someone else, my brother Franco, and he was smiling in that special way of his.

When we were about fourteen or fifteen years old, Franco and I began to do by ourselves what we had previously done with Dad: swing into action for alpine rescue maneuvers. He would hurry to get the person into a harness, while I nailed the spikes into the ice, arranged the carabiners, and pulled the rope. We saved many people that way. We became a well-oiled machine. Thinking back, I can feel the fear in the pit of my stomach, in my legs: we were alone, often at night, and the rocks looked like advancing soldiers. But we were never afraid back then: we did what we had to, without thinking about it.

But I felt actual terror, when a few months before my wedding Franco told me, "I went to have some tests done, because I always felt tired. I have leukemia." I stared at him in disbelief. "What do you mean, leukemia?"

Franco, the invincible, the one who never ran out of breath. "Forgive me, my love," I said to my Alba, "but instead of a honeymoon I'll have to be in the hospital. We'll make it up later." At the Niguarda hospital in Milan they did all of the tests and prepared me to give a little bit of my life to my brother, with a bone marrow transplant. I thought, "I'm still older, I'm the one who decides. And I have decided to save him, he'll have to deal with it." Afterward I went to Rome, to the tomb of my friend the pope beneath the Vatican, to pray with his rosary in my hand. It was the last one he had given to me, made of little opalescent and white stones. He didn't know what to say . . . he was silent. There is a niche in front of the tomb, in front of the sepulcher of the queen of Sweden who died at the end of the seventeenth century. I stood there watching the unending stream of people.

I left with my knees doubling from fear: I had understood, I had heard his voice speaking in me. Our dialogue still works, albeit at a distance. It has happened in these days in which I am unpacking these memories and putting them down on paper—I see him again in a thousand moments, in a thousand circumstances. It was his way of helping me, because he knew that Franco was a part of me.

Our little church in Temù was overflowing for Franco's funeral. I had composed some thoughts:

> It is true that love is discovered only by loving. And today, only today, I am realizing how much I loved you, how much we loved you. "Brothers" is a word that sums up so much, that encloses a world made up of many days, one after another, making up these years, these lives. I look back for a moment: we are still there on our Adamello. A span of ice glowing with the gentle pink light of sunset, and the two of us there. Silent, not speaking, but rather incessantly

engaged in doing: races, games, climbing, trees, stones, bonfires, downhill runs, all of it in an unbroken stream, all of it life to be gulped down greedily with the voracious presumption of youth. Our gym was that special world, with the endless skies capping those long days full of life, scents, tests, challenges, an enormous but unnoticed happiness that becomes clear to me only today.

You know, Franco, I don't think I ever told you this, but the most powerful, most beautiful emotions, those most rooted in memory, I experienced with you. In those sunny days up there where God made himself tree, mountain, stream, or flapping of wings. And I am sure that he was playing with us, too. I have always tried to protect you, even if I was only a year older than you, I was the grown-up, the trailblazer, but now I know that when I looked back it was from you that I regained the strength and the will to keep moving forward. You know that this time as well I tried to protect you. I did so without wavering—I hoped, I prayed, I wept.

So should I consider myself completely defeated now? No, indeed no. Because I loved you, and you loved me just as much. I know that I must not lack the courage to imagine you happy where you have gone. I seem to see you: those who went before you have come to welcome you, to celebrate your arrival. And then there was the hand of someone special, who lifted you up into the presence of God. He is still dressed in white, he was the pope of all, and all of us consider him a saint already. You know, Franco,

> I loved you, and I entrust you to him. While I will continue to think about you for all the days that are yet to come.

Dear reader, I have a question for you now: Do you know a mountain? No? Then seek one out, find it. Go to the summit, on a day on which it seems to you that you cannot make it. Seek out a place in which your eyes can delve into the absolute, in which the sky can be a private show for no one but you. Sit down. Breathe deeply the air as you have not done for some time. Savor it. Look in front of you, toward the infinite: and only then, prepare to throw away your anger, disappointment, fear, and discontent. They are useless burdens. Become silent, at one with the silence around you.

Wait with trust, and something will happen. Someone will listen to you. Do not ask, do not propose, do not think. Just listen. You will suddenly perceive; you will understand something that escaped you, something you didn't know you could count on. You will understand that you have a great fortune hidden in your pocket: your life, because you are in the world, and you are there . . . and this is no small thing. That beauty around you will suddenly touch your heart. It is yours, it belongs to you. You are its absolute master. And you are part of it. Do you believe, or do you not believe? It doesn't matter much, because it's true.

Seek the memory of him, seek his voice, seek his

smile. He will come. On earth he knew how to draw God down from heaven, he took him by the hand and brought him here. Keep a spot for him next to you, and keep waiting patiently. That spot will be your shrine, go back there as often as you need. He and the mountain will teach you to love, and to love yourself.

All of a sudden I feel an urgent need to be there again myself. To get there fast I take a cable car to the Passo Tonale, get off, and continue on foot. I start by crossing the glacier of Presena, come to the pass of Marocarro, and there the expanse of the perennial ice of Pian di Neve opens up. For a moment I am breathless. Then I breathe deeply and keep going: I go down to the valley, walking for a good hour, to the Mondrone Lodge.

Then the ascent rears up again, toward the Lobbia, toward home, toward the part of me that I always leave there. At a certain point, I leave the trail on the rocks and come to the final stretch—it is like going to visit a sweetheart, but it is the glacier that is waiting for me. I see the lodge, and it looks like a mirage, I keep walking and walking and walking, it seems I will never get there. It is as if it is making a game of eluding me.

When I think I can't go any further, it stops playing and consoles me, seeming to say, "Come on, come get me, I'm still here." Just a few hundred yards more over the sharp-edged stones of the moraine, and I'm there. I sit down and catch my breath on that bench, on that terrace looking out over the world. Suddenly evening has fallen. I look up, and stars are shining in that velvety blue. I look at them. It seems to me that I can recognize Betelgeuse, and then Sirius and Rigel.

And you? Are you watching me, Lolek? Are you watching me, Karol? Are you watching me, saint?

I close my eyes, and there you are. On this sliver of mountain you have left a sign . . . and it is a Cross.

# CHRONOLOGY OF EVENTS

On May 13, 1917 (note the date), in Fatima, the Blessed Mother appeared to the three *pastorinhos* Jacinta, Francisco, and Lucia.

On July 13, 1917, during the third apparition, the Blessed Mother revealed the secret to the children.

On January 3, 1941, the third part of the secret was written down at the order of His Excellency the bishop of Leiria.

In 1942, the first and second parts of the secret were revealed, which showed them the vision of hell, predicted the Soviet revolution, the Second World War, the expansion of communism, and the persecution of the Church. The third part of the secret remains shrouded in mystery. Only one manuscript exists, and in order to protect the secret better the envelope was delivered to the secret archive of the Holy Office on April 4, 1957.

On August 17, 1959, the commissioner of the Holy Office, Fr. Pierre Paul Philippe, brought Pope John

XXIII the envelope containing the third part of the "secret." His Holiness, after a bit of hesitation, said, "Let's wait. I will pray. I will let you know what I have decided."

In reality, Pope John XXIII decided to send the sealed envelope back to the Holy Office, and not to reveal the third part of the secret yet.

On March 27, 1965, Pope Paul VI read the contents together with His Excellency Archbishop Angelo dell'Acqua, and sent the envelope back to the archive of the Holy Office with the same decision not to publish the text.

On May 13, 1981, the world was in shock: in Saint Peter's Square, the pope was shot and critically wounded, and seemed to be saved only by an "odd" change of the bullet's trajectory.

On July 18, 1981, having recovered quickly from the tragic consequences of his injury, he had the two envelopes delivered to him (one containing the original drafted by Sister Lucia in Portuguese, the other with the Italian translation), read the contents, and kept them with him until August 11, the day on which he decided to send them back to the archive of the Holy Office. Once again, the highest confidentiality was observed concerning the "third secret."

On July 16, 1984, at 10:15 that Monday, Pope John Paul II and his friend, President Sandro Pertini, arrived on the Adamello. They were received in great secrecy by the Zani family, who had managed for many years the lodge dedicated to the soldiers who had fallen on the Adamello. The pope skied for an hour, guided by Lino Zani, his brother, and a few others.

Then he returned for lunch at the lodge, where Lino's mom had prepared a mixed antipasto of prosciutto, salami, and carpaccio, "strozzapreti" ("priest-chokers") (it was Perini who dared to make the joke, "Your Holiness, today we're going to do you in"), risotto, roast beef with salad, cheese, wild berries, and fruitcake. All washed down with white Tocai wine and local grappa.

After lunch, the pope said goodbye to Pertini (who was going back to Rome) and, again accompanied by Lino and by his security team, resumed skiing.

Upon reaching Cresta Croce, the pope passed a tower, part of the ruins of a fortified citadel built by the alpine soldiers during the bloody fighting of the First World War. From there he spotted a cross (the tower, which now functions as an observatory, is about a hundred meters away from the cross itself), formed by two trunks of rough-hewn wood, with the bark so discolored it looked like cork, identical to the description contained in the third secret. He was deeply moved, and asked

Lino how long that cross had been there, who had put it there, and if there really were many bodies of poor soldiers buried there. The soldiers had been killed not so much by the fighting as by the hardships, the lack of food and the cold. He recollected himself in prayer for quite some time. Then he asked for more information, and confided something to Lino: his father, Józef, had also fought under terrible conditions in that very same place, during the First World War. At 7:00 p.m. the pope, together with the little group, went back to the lodge run by the Zanis, where he was to spend the night.

Without a doubt, from that night on the pope was very closely bound to that territory, so much so as to ask that a large granite cross be made there with an altar, for the repose of those poor soldiers fallen and still buried beneath the perennial ice. (From time to time, in fact, the remains of soldiers reappear in that territory.)

In 1988, John Paul II returned there to bless the granite altar erected at 10,849 feet, right on Cresta Croce itself. A little further below there is still the 149G cannon brought there by the alpine soldiers in 1917, which became the symbol of that bloody combat.

On December 31, 1999, in the epochal transition of New Years, John Paul II reiterated the symbolic value of that altar and of that granite cross built on the Adamello with a religious ceremony broadcast worldwide.

On May 13, 2000, the pope went to Fatima to beatify Jacinta and Francisco, and it was Cardinal Angelo Sodano, the Vatican secretary of state, who made the official announcement: "As you know, the purpose of his visit to Fatima has been to beatify the two 'little shepherds.' Nevertheless he also wishes his pilgrimage to be a renewed gesture of gratitude to Our Lady for her protection during these years of his papacy. This protection seems also to be linked to the so-called 'third part' of the secret of Fatima."

On June 26, 2000, a press conference was held at the Vatican, at the end of which the third secret was "published," together with a commentary written by Cardinal Ratzinger and by then-archbishop Tarcisio Bertone, entitled *The Message of Fatima*. The contribution written by Cardinal Ratzinger and Archbishop Bertone affirms: "The decision of His Holiness Pope John Paul II to make public the third part of the 'secret' of Fatima brings to an end a period of history marked by tragic human lust for power and evil, yet pervaded by the merciful love of God and the watchful care of the Mother of Jesus and of the Church."

In 2003 came another gesture of high symbolic value: the pope had the first two medallions celebrating the twenty-fifth anniversary of his pontificate mounted at the foot of the monument erected on Cresta Croce. He placed the bullet from Agca's gun that was extracted from his body, into the crown of the Virgin of Fatima, and the bloody sash that he had been wearing around his waist on the day of the attack was given to the Polish shrine of Jasna Góra. This was another decision with an unmistakable meaning: Pope John Paul II, a man destined for a project of holiness.

On the verge of the beatification of Pope John Paul II, in May 2011, Lino Zani agreed to recount in its entirety, with faithful precision and a spirit of authentic and Christian awareness, the human and spiritual story that has bound him in a truly exceptional relationship with the pope most loved by the people, revisiting the trail of all the memories of those twenty-one extraordinary years with the Holy Father.

And above all, to bear witness to all that which, implicitly, induced John Paul II to exhort him, telling him first about his departure for one of the climbs above eight thousand meters (more precisely, that of the Tibetan peak of Cho Oyu): "You, Lino, must be our 'apostle of the mountains,' planting crosses on the highest summits, at every latitude, for the glory of the Lord."

And Lino Zani has obeyed, having a cross blessed by the pope at each one of his departures and carrying this symbol of Christianity all the way to the North Pole (an expedition made with Mike Bongiorno), fulfilling, in essence, this extraordinary commitment.

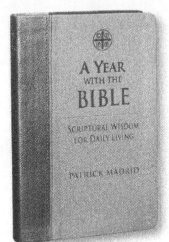